UNDERSTANDING PIETISM

UNDERSTANDING PIETISM

by

Dale W. Brown

William B. Eerdmans Publishing Company

To
Floyd E. Mallott
who first engendered
my interest in Pietism

Copyright © 1978 by Wm. B. Eerdmans Publishing Co.
255 Jefferson Ave. S.E., Grand Rapids, Mich. 49503
All rights reserved
Printed in the United States of America

Library of Congress Cataloging in Publication Data

Brown, Dale W., 1926-
   Understanding pietism.

   1. Pietism—History.   I. Title.
BR1650.2.B76   273'.7   77-29104
ISBN 0-8028-1710-6 pbk.

Contents

Preface

As a graduate student more than a decade ago, I found myself in the thick of a neo-orthodox atmosphere dominated by the theology of Luther, Calvin, Brunner, Barth, Kierkegaard, and Bonhoeffer. I had been taught that my own denomination, the Church of the Brethren, had Pietist origins, and I became interested in the frequency with which the word "pietist" was used disparagingly. I began to question professors, lecturers, and fellow students: "What did you mean when you applied the label 'pietist'?" The replies indicated hostility and no small amount of confusion. Pietism connoted subjectivism, individualism, and otherworldliness.

For my doctoral dissertation, I was interested in the fascinating radical Pietist Gottfried Arnold, who wrote a massive three-volume church history, *Unparteyische Kirchen und Ketzer Historie,* which purported to be impartial in demonstrating that the true church has often been preserved by schismatics and alleged heretics. In order to acquire background for this research, I felt it necessary to learn something of the mainline Pietist movement led by Spener and Francke. I became stuck there because I discovered in English historiography a tremendous void in the treatment of Pietism. My dissertation,

"The Problem of Subjectivism in Pietism: A Redefinition with Special Reference to the Theology of Philipp Jakob Spener and August Hermann Francke" (Evanston, Garrett Theological Seminary and Northwestern University, 1962), was intended to help fill this gap.

Since writing my dissertation, I have continued research in Germany and have conversed with other students of Pietism in order to evaluate some of my conclusions. The present book reflects that further study.

I want to thank the faculty and students of North Park Seminary for invaluable criticisms of ideas I presented in lectures there. It was also helpful to participate with the ministers of the Evangelical Covenant Church in an ashram devoted to discussing the relevance of historic Pietist motifs for lay people. Then, too, I wish to express appreciation to my students at Bethany Theological Seminary, who have been helpful in formulating the issues, interpretations, and critiques offered in this book. Finally, may I commend the editors of *The Covenant Quarterly* for maintaining an interest in Pietism by publishing articles in this area even when it was not in vogue to do so. Thanks in part to their efforts, a movement of which few people were more than vaguely aware a decade ago is now attracting much attention.

Dale W. Brown

1

Pietism: What Is It?

Pietism has been one of the least understood movements in Judeo-Christian history. Despite Pietism's tremendous influence on Christian life in the United States, the lack of Pietist studies constitutes one of the greatest gaps in American church historiography. This void may partially account for the misunderstanding described by Paul Tillich:

> What is Pietism? The term is much less respectable in America than in Europe. There the words "pious" and "pietist" can be used of people, but hardly in America, because here they carry the connotations of hypocrisy and moralism. Pietism does not necessarily have these connotations.[1]

Though little understood, the word is appropriated in various ways, with a multiplicity of connotations, and consequently we must examine these and begin to work at clarifying definitions.

Negative and Positive Assessments

Many twentieth-century theologians have used "Pietism" as a swearword to blast undesirable theological tendencies. Though he later exhibited more balance in understanding, Barth's early aversion seemed to set the tone for mainline theologians: "Better with the Church in hell than with pietists, of higher or lower type — in a heaven which does not exist."[2] In twentieth-century theological parlance, Pietism has been identified negatively as emotionalism, mysticism, rationalism, subjectivism, asceticism, quietism, synergism, chiliasm, moralism, legalism, separatism, individualism, and otherworldliness. Such characterizations in many ways echo the polemical utterances of the Pietists' early orthodox opponents who called them, among other names: Donatists, Pelagians, Albigenses, Rosicrucians, Schwenkfeldians, Weigelians, Osiandrians, Syncretists, Majorists, Quakers, and Enthusiasts. Though subsequent historical assessments have featured fewer such heretical tags, the consensus of many historians would be reflected in Martin Marty's analysis: "For all its glories, Pietism was one of the major strides of Christian retreat from responsibility as it has been viewed in the past."[3]

Protagonists have surrounded Pietism with other connotations: integrity, goodness, and holistic responses in terms of life styles; regeneration, sanctification, holiness, and the work of the Spirit in the context of biblical themes; and freedom, charity, tolerance, and equality in the areas of ecumenism and mission. Historians have credited the movement with fostering some of the good ingredients of the Enlightenment, German Idealism, Romanticism, the Great Awakening, revivalism, many new denominations, the worldwide missionary movement of the nineteenth century, and many kinds of philanthropic activity. F. Ernest Stoeffler regards Pietism as the most dynamic movement within Protestantism.[4] Donald Bloesch evaluates Pietism as being one of the "wellsprings of new life in the church" and as contributing those who "are in the vanguard of what might be considered radical or revolutionary Christianity."[5]

The same diametrically opposite assessments are revealed in theological analyses. Pietism has been criticized for its development of anthropological centers and normative programmed conversion experiences; it has been heralded for its frequent revival of emphasis on the Holy Spirit. Pietism has been deplored because of its simplistic classification of people as regenerate or unregenerate; it has been praised for its recovery of the biological metaphor of regeneration as a valid supplement to the juridical metaphor of justification. Pietism has been accused of extreme subjectivism in exegesis and a subversive undermining of creeds and ecclesiastical authority; it has been regarded as a vital expression of the doctrine of the priesthood of all believers. Pietism has been charged with devaluation of culture, focus on adiaphora, and preoccupation with private virtues; it has been commended for its missionary efforts, ecumenism, and charitable fruits.

These ambiguous interpretations are consistent with the etymology of the root word "piety." The most cited New Testament synonym for piety is *eusebeia*, which means "reverence" and is often translated as "godliness." The Latin, *pietas*, points to filial affection for the family of God. The English word "piety" signals pity and compassion. And the German, *fromm*, can mean either "godly and devout" or "gentle, harmless, and simple." In addition to favorable interpretations, the word has long carried negative connotations. For example, II Timothy 3:5 states that it is possible to have the form of *eusebeia* while denying the power of it. A pious person can be marked by devoutness in worship and conduct, or piety can refer to one whose actions are marked by self-conscious virtue, conspicuous religiosity, or hypocrisy.

Nevertheless, piety and Pietism are not to be completely equated. Pietism represents one of the historic forms of piety which are a part of our heritage. *Pietismus* (the German word) was an uncomplimentary nickname bequeathed to posterity by Pietism's detractors. The idea for the name might have come from Philipp Jakob Spener's *Pia Desideria,* a preface to Johann Arndt's "Church Postil" which set forth Spener's devout wishes for the reformation of the church. The publication of this preface in 1675 is regarded as the precipitating event in the birth of German Pietism. Or the idea for the word might have come from the conventicles called *collegia pietatis* ("study classes in piety") first suggested by Spener in 1669 following one of his sermons dealing with false righteousness. When some of his Frankfurt parishioners queried, "What can we do?", Bible study and fellowship groups were inaugurated. Spener's perspective on the origin of the name is revealed in his description of the critics: "Those who feared through such holiness to have their own deeds put to shame began to call in mockery, 'Pietists!' (which name soon spread)."[6] The opponents, no doubt, were attacking the special claim and the kind of piety which they associated with the groups. Our earliest record of the name "Pietists" indicates that it first appeared at Darmstadt in 1677. Although Spener advised the groups to bear in patience what had been dubbed by opponents, he wrote, "I hope that no one

among us or our acquaintances or our friends has at any
time used this name for himself."[7]
Others were not as reluctant to accept the designation.
The name gained its greatest repute during an outbreak
of disputes at the University of Leipzig. August Hermann
Francke had been a leading participant in a *collegium
philobiblicum*, a conventicle formed for the purpose of en-
tering more deeply into edifying exegesis. The numbers and
enthusiasm of students and citizens grew to the extent
that the authorities investigated and forbade such assem-
blies in an electoral edict on March 10, 1690. At a funeral
for one of the "awakened" students, one of Francke's faculty opponents, Johann Carpzov, gave evidence of his dis-
pleasure with the movement: "Our mission as professors
is to make students more learned and not more pious."[8]
In response, poetry professor Joachim Feller was one of
the first to favorably define and identify himself with the
name. His definition is found in his poem of 1689:

> *The name of the Pietists is now known all*
> *over town.*
> *Who is a Pietist? He who studies the*
> *Word of God*
> *And accordingly leads a holy life.*
> *This is well done, good for every Christian.*
> *For this amounts to nothing if after the manner*
> *of rhetoricians*
> *And disputants one puts on airs in the pulpit*
> *And does not live holy as one ought*
> *according to the teaching.*
> *Piety above all must rest in the heart.*[9]

In a second poem, Feller is not ashamed to call himself a
Pietist:

> *The pietists of our day*
> *Are Christians given wholly*
> *To kindness, love, and truth; and they*
> *Are striving to be holy.*
> *I will confess that I embrace*
> *Their doctrine of salvation*
> *Without restraint or any trace*
> *Of shame and hesitation.*[10]

All such equivocal attitudes toward Pietism substantiate the observation of Egon Gerdes that the problem of Pietism may be, to a great extent, semantic. In his excellent article "Pietism: Classical and Modern,"[11] he compares Feller's description as found in the above poems with a contemporary description of the "pious" as humorously delineated in Charles Merrill Smith's *How to Become a Bishop without Being Religious.*[12] Whereas Feller regarded the Pietist as one who did not represent the hypocrisy of his orthodox opponent, Smith sees the "pious image" as the phony, respectable posture which does not characterize the genuinely religious man. For Feller, the Pietist was the "good guy" applying his doctrine to life. For Smith, the pious constitute the "bad guys" who with their heads in the clouds of lofty thoughts disengage themselves from the secular concerns of humanity. Gerdes uses this contrast as a case study to demonstrate how the attack on modern Pietism is often fought with weapons from the arsenal of classical Pietism.[13] Because of the frequency of this language discrepancy, some have spoken of our usage as the "bogey of Pietism."[14]

This twentieth-century propensity to define Pietism primarily in the context of its caricatures and degenerate legacies is being altered by an increasing amount of interest and research. The recent renaissance of Pietist studies in Europe is beginning to spill over to America. Along with the negative connotations which regularly mark theological discussions, there are appearing more positive evaluations through the work of scholars such as F. Ernest Stoeffler, Theodore Tappert, Egon Gerdes, Alter Kukkonen, James Bemesderfer, James Tanis, Allen Deeter, John Weborg, and the faculty of North Park Theological Seminary.

Historical Context

Even when we make the case that Pietism as a historical movement is to be differentiated from other manifestations of piety and many contemporary caricatures, there remains a major problem of historiography. Is Pietism to be defined only as that movement in the last quarter of seventeenth-century and first half of eighteenth-century Germany which revolved around the reform activity of Spener and Francke? Or are we to adopt a broader understanding identifying Pietism as a major Protestant movement which has roots in Bucer's mediating position between Luther and Calvin and in mystical and sectarian streams; which was manifested first in English Puritanism and Dutch Reformed circles and appeared in Lutheranism through Arndt, Spener, Francke, Bengel, Zinzendorf, and a host of others; which was radicalized by people like Gottfried Arnold, Ernst Hochmann, Johann K. Dippel, and the Petersens, was romanticized by Jung-Stilling, and was appropriated by Moravians, the Church of the Brethren, Swedish Mission Friends, the Wesleyan movement, and the evangelical revivals; and which continues as the basic religious ethos of a host of organizations, societies, and denominations?[15] Our understanding will be helped most by incorporating a bit of truth from each of these positions. It is important to recognize motifs and manifestations shared by German Pietism and much that preceded and followed. The intimate relationships between the movements and their common group of emphases have produced characteristics which still exist and which can be properly labeled as pietistic. Nevertheless, we must use a more narrow definition in order to avoid semantic problems. Specific names such as Reformed Pietism, Radical Pietism, Moravianism, English Evangelicalism, Methodism, and the Great Awakening designate the varieties of historical manifestations. Because the etymology of "Pietism" emerged in the German context, there is a certain logic in assuming that the word used alone refers to the Spener-Francke axis. The movements which historians call Reform Pietism came first but were only given the Pietist label after the struggles within German Lutheranism. Other movements such as Methodism and the Anglo-American Awakenings quickly emerged from the same milieu, but they were different enough from classical Pietism to be called cousins rather than sisters or brothers.

This study, therefore, will primarily use the name Pietism in the more narrow sense and apply specific labels when referring to kindred movements. That we cannot be entirely consistent in this bears witness that the word has taken on many additional historical accretions. Whichever way we look at the phenomena, our understanding of all pietistic tendencies will be enhanced through a brief look at the historical roots and the sociological and religious milieu of German Pietism.

Roots

(1) *Luther.* The early Pietists espoused continuity with Luther and reform orthodoxy. Pietist writings were replete with quotations from the father of the Reformation, with special emphasis on the young Luther's use of personal pronouns and his description of faith as a dynamic force which works through love. From his teacher Johann Dannhauer, Spener gained a thorough and appreciative knowledge of Luther. Others among Spener's teachers represented the reform party which had deplored many departures from Luther and advocated reforms such as increased lay participation and greater knowledge of Scripture, concerns which were later formulated by Spener in his *Pia Desideria*.

(2) *Calvinism.* The genesis of German Pietism owes much to the Reformed tradition, particularly to its Puritan strands. Though it is an overstatement to define Pietism as emerging entirely from the impact of Calvinism on Lutheran soil, the Calvinistic stress on moral earnestness, biblicism, and more democratic polity were later to become basic to Pietism. It is likely that Spener derived the idea of the conventicle as a medium of reform from Martin Bucer, whose Reformed tendencies were prevalent at Strasbourg when Spener studied there. By the age of fourteen Spener had read Lewis Bayly's *Praxis Pietatis* ("Practice of Piety") as well as other English Puritan devotional works by Dyke, Sonthom, and Baxter. Such Puritan literature, focusing on the conscience, the scrutinization of

daily life, and the formulation of rules of living, was eagerly received in Pietist circles. Pietistic manifestations emerged in seventeenth-century Holland through Teelinck and his mysticism, Voet and his disciplined conventicles which spawned the movement called Precisianism, Koch and his covenant biblical theology, Lodensteyn and his more charismatic conventicles, and Labadie (who had a profound influence on young Spener) and his radical and separatist tendencies. The impact of these Dutch reform activities spilled over onto German terrain, and historians have confirmed the similarity of the Dutch experience to what was to occur later in Germany by attaching the name Reformed Pietism to the movement.

(3) *Mysticism.* Streams of spiritualism and mysticism have been among the most frequently cited sources of both Dutch and German Pietism. Though this influence has been overemphasized by some historians, most agree with Eric Seeberg's assertion that "there is a streak of mysticism in all Pietism."[16] Spener possessed little natural inclination for mysticism in his preoccupation with practical Christianity, but he did maintain an openness to mystical theology and a feeling that mystical literature was helpful for personal piety even though it was not always sound in doctrine. Luther's own promotion of the medieval mystical tract *Theologia Germanica* was often cited in defense of these interests. Many scholars have followed Albrecht Ritschl in his major thesis that Pietism represented the renewal in the Lutheran Church of the mystical folk movement of the thirteenth century.[17] Any such dependence on medieval currents was certainly supplemented by the influence of spiritualist representatives of the left wing Re-

formation such as Kaspar Schwenkfeld, Andreas Osiander, and Valentin Weigel. A generation later the lay shoemaker of Görlitz, Jakob Boehme (1575-1624), cast nature mysticism in a Lutheran mold. His concept of the will and his emphasis on freedom became basic to later German philosophy. His empathy for the world bequeathed an ethical mysticism to many varieties of disciples. And his pacifism, universalism, and spiritualistic interpretations of the church have been considered by many as seminal to Radical Pietism. One of his contemporaries, the Lutheran churchman Johann Arndt, is often regarded as the father of Pietism before Spener. Arndt's *True Christianity* (1605), which was important to Spener and widely used in Pietist circles, evoked controversy concerning whether it was truly evangelical or tainted with Roman Catholic mysticism. Arndt and his circle, including men like Johann Andrea and the popular hymn writer, Paul Gerhardt, can also be placed with the reform orthodox party because of their concern over the corruption of the church. Francke and his followers were attracted to the so-called southern type of mysticism of Spain, especially that of Miguel de Molinos. This movement, which included Teresa of Avila and John of the Cross in Spain and Francis de Sales and Madame Guyon in France, stressed the need to cultivate a freedom from excessive love for the things of this world.

(4) *Sects.* Albrecht Ritschl considered mystical and sectarian motifs to be closely related. Many have followed his lead, seeing Pietism as the revival of medieval and Reformation sectarianism.[18] Historically, Pietism emerged when much of the zeal had departed from the Anabaptist movement, flourishing best on Anabaptist soil and finding

strength in Anabaptist strongholds such as Württemberg. The common people often used the names Pietists and Anabaptists synonymously. Pietists read widely in *Das Geistliche Blumengärtlein*, which contained writings by Hans Denck, Hans Hut, Jorg Hauck von Jackson, and Eitelhaus Langelmantel. Radical Pietist Gottfried Arnold, in his monumental *Impartial History of the Church and Heretics*,[19] was one of the first to evaluate Anabaptism in light of the primary source materials rather than the customary polemical works of its opponents. Anabaptism and Pietism shared the desire to carry the Reformation to its logical conclusion. They held in common a belief in the guidance of the Holy Spirit, who taught correct understanding of the Scriptures; the idea of the restoration of the primitive church; the centrality of *Wiedergeburt* ("new birth"); and the ethical motifs of *Nachfolge Christi* ("imitation of Christ"), the Sermon on the Mount, and the Christian life as a fruit of faith.

Though Spener coveted for the Lutherans the almost blameless life style of nearby Mennonites, he disagreed in certain matters of doctrine. From the other side, Anabaptist scholars have felt that for the Pietists the new birth meant a peaceful possession and an assurance of individual salvation, whereas for the Anabaptists it meant following after Christ even in suffering. In contrast to the strong Anabaptist emphasis on the gathered church, Pietist conventicles have been described as the gathering of the regenerate more for edification of individuals than for corporate obedience and discipline.[20] Basic ecclesiological differences were analyzed by Troeltsch in his classic descriptions of church, sect, and mystic types in Christendom. He classified Pietism as the appearance of a sect within the church.[21] The mainstream of classical Pietism, in contradistinction to Radical Pietism, sought to achieve reform within the church. For many, Pietism represents a milder and tamer descendant of the sects.

Social Milieu

Sociologically, Pietism was in many ways a moral reaction against the decadence resulting from the devastating Thirty Years' War, which concluded with the signing of the Treaty of Westphalia in 1648. Until the middle of the nineteenth century, scarcely any estimate of loss of life and wealth was too extravagant for belief. The population was said to have decreased by three quarters; the loss in livestock and wealth was even greater. Because of the exaggerations in documents drawn up by people attempting to obtain financial help, there has long been a need for historical revisionism in the study of the effects of the war. More recently some have revised the revisionists, who perhaps overly minimized the extent of the destruction. Whatever the interpretation, the war left a unique psychological impact upon its survivors and their posterity. Never before had there been such a universal sense of irretrievable disaster. The war was religiously divisive, morally subversive, economically destructive, socially degrading, and ultimately futile in its results.

The war left the Germanies fragmented with princes, cities, and principalities who determined the religious affiliation of their constituents. If one did not share the confession of the ruler (which according to the treaty was required to be Catholic, Lutheran, or Reformed), his only options were persecution or emigration. A few princes did grant religious freedom in order to attract settlers to their depopulated areas. Unfortunately, the end of the war did not bring peace. The power struggle which developed between the Hapsburgs of Austria and the royal house of France meant that German territories were constantly subject to advancing and retreating armies. This turbulent condition continued until the end of the seventeenth century.

Pietism gained its strongest footholds in the cities which had fared the best economically, Frankfurt, Hamburg, and Dresden, but the conditions were still such that the Pietist reformers attacked the vulgarity, brutality, and coarseness of the masses as well as the prevalent immorality in high places of church and state. The interest in peace and pacifism in Pietist circles can probably be traced to the anti-war sentiment which usually follows the cessation of an unpopular war. Pietism arose in the context of a widespread espousal of sorcery, alchemy, exorcism, and capital punishment for witches. It should be added, however, that this was also a time which witnessed new intellectual ferment and the advent of the age of science. Pietism did not escape some of these newer currents: for his master's thesis, Spener wrote a metaphysical and ethical critique of Thomas Hobbes's authoritarian and utilitarian principles; and Francke frequently found himself in dialogue with Leibniz.

Unlike Methodism in England, however, Pietism was not so much a reaction to the irreligious currents of the scientific revolution and the Enlightenment as to the religious milieu within its own Lutheran Church. More than just a protest against the moral decadence, the caesaropapism, and the polemical spirit emanating from the bitter religious war, Pietism was also a reaction to the theological methods and creedal rigidity of what Pietists felt to be a "dead" Orthodoxy. Although Luther had repudiated rationalism and philosophical roads to God, his insistence on correct doctrine was no doubt an impetus to the rise of Lutheran Orthodoxy. His rejection of Scholasticism, the method and teaching of the medieval Schoolmen, was soon tempered by the more irenic and systematic mind of his humanist associate, Melanchthon. Second-generation Lutherans found it imperative to defend "pure doctrine" from the onslaughts of zealous Calvinists and the crusading spirit of the Jesuits. The resulting movement, which has been known as Protestant Orthodoxy or Protestant Scholasticism, is as difficult to define as Pietism because of the inability to pinpoint the movement to any one person, the widespread varieties of expression, and the great number of controversies which raged within its fold. The resolution of the many theological disputes came from Martin Chemnitz and Jacob Andreae's reworking the creedal contributions of Luther, Melanchthon, and Brenz. The resulting Formula of Concord, which constituted the creedal or Symbolical Books of Lutheranism, was circulated for approval and received the signatures of thousands, primarily pastors, teachers, electors, princes, counts, and city authorities. Following this consensus, which embraced the majority of Lutheran territories in Germany, the Scholastic period flourished in the seventeenth century, reaching its greatest influence in the middle of the century through three Protestant Scholastics — J. F. Koenig, John

Andrew Quenstedt, and Abraham Calovius — and finding its strictest and strongest center at the University of Wittenberg.

Positively, this movement toward Orthodoxy can be viewed as faith seeking understanding, the necessity for a young and growing Lutheranism to define itself amid political maneuverings and theological cleavages. Orthodoxy retained a reform party and some who shared Luther's suspicion of philosophy. It should be kept in mind that many of the caricatures and criticisms of Orthodoxy by Pietists were directed more against its extremes and degenerations than against its solid center and finest representatives.

Negatively, some have felt that in Protestant Scholasticism we have an "intellectual Pelagianism" in which the good works of the medieval church were exchanged for the works of understanding. Aristotle, who had been thrown out the front door, quickly came in the back. Justification by faith became one of the dogmas instead of the source of dogma. Luther's God, who was a Thou, became an It. The testimony of the Holy Spirit became a mere intellectual process of increasing acquaintance with the truth. Though there was an apotheosis of the Bible, the Scriptures were used primarily as proof texts to verify the creedal dogmas.

The Pietists became most vocal against what they regarded to be the practical results. They reacted against the many long series of polemical sermons which opposed all non-Lutheran positions as well as against the strong weight placed on rhetoric and learning. They were dismayed over the decline in catechetical instruction, the de-emphasis of prayer, and the priority which the study of theology assumed over exegesis in the universities. They claimed that correct doctrine did not seem to make a difference in the morality and lives of all those who possessed it.

In spite of the inroads of the Pietist reformation, Protestant Scholasticism continued as a dominant theological and political influence well into the early decades of the eighteenth century. It was to be the *Aufklärung* ("German Enlightenment") which would seriously challenge both Orthodox and Pietist dominance. Pietism has been charged or credited with the rise of German Rationalism due to its subversion of objective authority and because of its easy movement from the focus on "the inner light" to "the flash of insight." On the other hand, it has been asserted that the extreme intellectualism of late Orthodoxy might have prepared the way for the Age of Reason. Whatever the analysis, it is interesting that in later eighteenth- and nine-tenth-century manifestations of conservative Protestantism, one often finds the merger of what had previously been the sharp opposing strands of Orthodoxy and Pietism.

It is important to keep in mind that the struggles within the Lutheran church in Germany were not isolated from a larger spectrum of kindred religious movements. Elsewhere there were zealous reactions to excessive tradition-alism, rigid institutionalism, and the Enlightenment which appeared in France and England before appearing in Germany. Contrary to our more narrow delimitation, broader definitions of Pietism encompass other efforts to return to the religion of the heart. In its period of greatest influence, Jansenism was contemporaneous with German Pietism, and the strict moral standards and conventicle-like position of the Jansenists within French Roman Catholicism were similar to those in strict Puritanism and Pietism. Substituting the Fathers for the authority of the Bible, Jansenism was in some respects to Catholicism what Pietism was to Lutheranism. Another reaction to the ecclesiastical dogmatism of the Jesuits was Quietism under the leadership of the Spanish mystic Miguel de Molinos, whose *Spiritual Guide* was published in the same year as Spener's *Pia Desideria* (1675). In spite of their opposition to both Jansenism and Quietism, the Jesuits did spawn their own type of heart religion in the supreme devotion which surfaced in the Sacred Heart of Jesus, a special form of the older Bernardine Jesus-mysticism. Marguerite Marie Alacoque's ecstasy, in which she was allowed to rest her head upon the heart of Jesus, occurred in 1675, the year which is usually given as the birth date of German Pietism. Her fervent mystical devotion spread rapidly and even gained the special sanction of the papacy.

Not only west of the Rhine but in eastern Europe, not only in Christian circles but in Judaism, there were stirrings which shared the same *Zeitgeist* as Pietism. In the face of bitter persecution at the hands of traditional rabbinism emerged a popular Hasidic (the Hebrew root word for piety) movement which swept through eastern Jewry and the communities of Poland in the eighteenth and nineteenth centuries. One of its leading founders, Rabbi Israel ben Eliezer, lived during the same years as his Pietist counterpart, Zinzendorf (1700-1760). In our time this obscure movement has been resuscitated by Martin Buber and others who identify strongly with its mysticism, which hallows community and everyday life rather than withdrawing from them, "for man cannot love God in truth without loving the world."[22]

Central Theological Motifs

In subsequent chapters we will define more thoroughly the central theological motifs of the early movement. For now it will suffice to list those motifs in order to gain an initial overview and understanding.

First is a concern for the *reformation of the church*. Believing the first Reformation had bogged down in dogmatics, polemics, and institutional rigidity, the Pietists offered concrete proposals for Bible study, conventicles, and increased lay participation. This focus on practical Christianity may be indicative that Pietism fostered no theology of its own; however, the emphasis on practice, exegesis, and mystical appropriation of the grace of God often assumed and represented certain theological presuppositions.

A second theme is *emphasis on the Bible* — the means for the reformation of the church. The Pietists often shared with the sects the primitivist conviction that we are to be faithful to the New Testament by returning to the ways of the New Testament church. The Bible is to be read devotionally and appropriated in terms of life styles.

A third fundamental motif which emerges is the insistence that the reformation of doctrine which was inaugurated by Luther must be carried over into the *reformation of life*. Orthodoxy must be accompanied by *orthopraxis* ("right living"). The conviction that faith must become active in love and the focus on sanctification and godliness meant that Pietism was permeated at its core with an ethical flavor. Pictism usually represents an expression of a theology of goodness.

An integrally related fourth motif is the *theology of experience*. Martin Schmidt and others have maintained that the heart of Pietist theology is its focus on regeneration. Pietists strongly emphasized that the God who is good enough to forgive us is powerful enough to change us. Consequently, we find varying degrees of emphasis on repentance, the new birth, and conversion. In the revival of the doctrine of the Holy Spirit which usually accompanies any theology of experience in the biblical context, there appear the corollary accents on the importance of decision, on openness to the present and future, on voluntary response versus compulsion, and on persuasion rather than force in matters of religion.

Fifth, the Pietists had *hope for the world*. In spite of their opposition to many degenerate currents of the fallen world, Pietists expressed their love for the world through works of mercy and their hope for the world through an eschatology which expected a revolutionary transformation of the world to be accomplished by God's work in changing human lives.

Before expanding these themes into chapters, we need to look more carefully at the fundamental theological problem which has always plagued Pietism and its students and critics.

The Focus on Subjectivity

"Ach euer schrecklicher Subjektivismus!" ("Ah, your

dreadful subjectivism!")[23] is the first and most general charge which is raised against Pietists. Most other criticisms can be subsumed under this one. Subjectivism is the shifting of focus from outside of self to one's self. Theologically it has often connoted the exaltation of self in rebellion against God. It is the creating of a god or gods by the self. In this way revelation, tradition, and historical norms are minimized or replaced by moralism (the justification of self through works) or religious empiricism (the apprehension of God through feelings and experience). In any delineation of pietist characteristics, the appearance of terms such as personal, individualism, inwardness, heart, internalization, experience, feeling, emotions, mysticism, asceticism, separatism, and conversion points to subjectivism as one of the dominant themes and problems in the formulation of the theology of Pietism. Were the Pietist's anti-ecclesiastical tendencies of conventicle-like behavior and purist psychology guilty of undermining the authority and corporate nature of the church? Did the Pietist stress on the inner versus the outer Word and on the internal testimony of the Holy Spirit lead to the perils of private interpretation? Did the centering on regeneration and the shift from justification to sanctification tend to make a god of goodness instead of reflecting the goodness of God? Was the Holy Spirit reduced to a projection of the human spirit, and was an emotional state viewed as a means to faith instead of as the fruit of faith? Did Pietism's otherworldliness result in a preoccupation with personal religion, or did the emphasis on works of charity reflect a kingdom theology? These issues, which evolve from the problem of subjectivism, provide the framework for the bulk of our study.

A better understanding of Pietism will emerge from reflecting on the above questions in the light of the theology of the early movement and with special, though not exclusive, reference to Spener and Francke. This is only to adopt the stance of historiography used by others. Just as it would not be fair or accurate to define Lutheranism in terms of later Lutheran Scholasticism or even later Pietism, neither would it be fair to define Pietism by looking only at current manifestations of the movement. To define Lutheranism one must study Luther and his work, and likewise, to define Pietism we must begin by looking at its founders and their intentions. Since more extensive biographical data is available in other places,[24] brief sketches of the two dominant leaders, Spener and Francke, will be provided here only for the purpose of adding to the context of our analysis.

Philipp Jakob Spener (1635-1705) is considered by many to be the second most important personality to shape German Protestantism. This "patriarch of Pietism" was nurtured devoutly in the womb of the church. His godmother, Countess Agathe of Rappoltstein, in her piety and personal affection, stamped a permanent influence upon his life. Through her tutelage, the young boy read and absorbed popular Puritan and German devotional literature. From the age of twelve to fifteen Spener was more formally tutored by the court preacher, Joachim Stoll, who spent much time with him. Stoll, no doubt, was responsible for transmitting to his student the spirit of many of his own reform orthodox ideas. Later in life, when Baron von Canstein inquired whether Spener had ever been bad, the latter confessed "Indeed I was bad," and substantiated his answer by relating how at the age of twelve he was induced to join a dance and was so overtaken by fear that he ran away never to dance again.[25] The father of Pietism knew no dramatic conversion experience, and his life was free from many of the customary stresses and strains. As a student at Strasbourg, his work under excellent professors was exemplary. His life was somewhat secluded from other students, and at the end of his academic career he married a twenty-year-old girl recommended by his mother. His primary secular diversions consisted of his special interests in heraldry and German history.

Professionally, Spener was successful from the beginning. While finishing his doctoral work, an exegesis on the book of Revelation, he assumed some pastoral duties in Strasbourg. Subsequently, when he was called to become senior minister at Frankfort-on-the-Main (1666-1686), he was placed above colleagues twice his age. Serving as court chaplain at Dresden (1686-1691), he knew tension with the electoral prince, who was often drunk and only appeared to hear eight sermons in five years. Spener ended his career as the influential provost of St. Nicholas Church in Berlin and the official inspector of Prussian churches.

Possessing a deep pastoral interest, Spener preached simply and exegetically from carefully prepared manuscripts, wrote gentle rebuttals of his opponent's ideas, and engaged in a voluminous correspondence as the spiritual father of nearly all German Pietists. He remained active

and influential throughout his life. He rose daily at
5:30 a.m. for prayer and work. The correspondences in
which he had exchanged views and advice with all classes
of people were gathered near the end of his life in his
four-volume *Theologische Bedencken*. Spener's crucial role
in the development of Pietism can be seen in his published works, which number over one hundred; in his relationship with Francke, who as a young man had visited
in his home for two months; and in the fact that he was
chosen to be Zinzendorf's godfather. For his funeral
Spener requested a white robe and coffin as a symbol of
his eschatological hope for better times for the church.

August Hermann Francke (1663-1727) has been regarded as the Melanchthon of the Pietist reformation —
the volatile and controversial organizing genius of the
movement which had been fathered by the more irenic,
mild-mannered Spener. His devout mother, widowed when
he was very young, raised him at Gotha in an atmosphere
which emphasized the reform school of thought. Francke
read Arndt's *True Christianity* at an early age and was
tutored in Bible study by an older sister. At the age of
eleven he was given a special room for prayer. Shortly
thereafter, however, Francke became quite unruly and
full of mischief. He studied at Erfurt and Kiel, where he
excelled in languages, and he went on to earn a Master
of Arts degree at Leipzig. Though the Bible study groups
at Leipzig formed the context for his conversion, it required an intense anxiety and the example and teaching
of Spener to bring Francke to faith. When he was asked
to preach a sermon in Lüneberg in 1687, Francke experienced the terrible fear that he did not have the faith he

was attempting to set forth. Francke was magnetized by his visit with Spener the following year. He shared in the devotional life of the home, participated in Spener's struggles with the prince at Dresden, and helped with the endless correspondence. Vigorous activity and a series of bans by the authorities followed his visit. At Leipzig, the conventicles were forbidden. Francke retreated to his birthplace, Lübeck, to visit relatives and was forbidden to preach there. Appointed assistant minister at Erfurt in 1690, he experienced the success of large crowds. But the opposition also increased, and he was removed from office following a ministry of fifteen months.

Spener, who through his influence in the court of Brandenburg was beginning to pack the newly formed University of Halle with Pietist appointees, came to his rescue. In 1691 Francke was called to be pastor in the suburban church in Glaucha, and was also appointed to serve as professor of Greek and Oriental languages at the university. This inaugurated a career of thirty-six years as pastor, theologian, and founder of *Stiftungen* ("philanthropic institutions"). He nurtured biblical societies and a monthly periodical, "Biblical Observations," and served as a dominant influence on hundreds of divinity students who matriculated annually. His greatest innovations resulted from applying his pastoral concerns to the *Stiftungen* by using the divinity students as tutors, teachers, houseparents, and laborers. The poor-school which Francke founded soon evolved into a famous orphanage, a *Pädagogium* for upper-class students, a Latin School, a chemical laboratory, a bookstore, a home for indigent widows, a

home for itinerant beggars, a Bible institute for the printing
and distribution of Bibles, a laundry, a farm, and a brewery. As a result, Halle is often heralded as the point of
origination for inner missions (ministry to social needs),
foreign missions, and Jewish missions, for dissemination of
the Bible and other literature, and for the spread of Pietism
by young men who followed German soldiers and settle-
ments to eastern and southeastern Europe, North America
(especially Pennsylvania and Georgia), and many other
parts of the world.

We will refer primarily to the thought and works of
Spener and Francke and will focus mainly on the early
movement in our effort to understand Pietism. Though
the founders of Pietism have been remembered more as
practical reformers than as systematic theologians, it is
possible to deduce from their voluminous correspondence
and many other writings some of the theological presuppositions which undergirded their practical activities.
This is easier to do with the scholarly, methodical Spener
than with the action-oriented Francke. Occasionally we
will utilize the thought of Radical Pietists such as Gottfried Arnold in order to compare the early movement with
more radical manifestations. In the light of these early
leaders we will examine the validity of the charge of subjectivism in the major areas of ecclesiology, exegesis, ethics,
experience, and eschatology.

II

Individualism and Ecclesiology: The Doctrine of the Church

From the earliest conventicles to the present variety of charismatic and evangelical devotional groups, "pietistic" and "individualistic" have often been used synonymously in theological parlance. A seventeenth-century Pietist reported in his autobiography that his father admonished, "Whoever wants to get to Heaven, must act as if he were alone."[1] Did Pietism so shift the focus to individual soteriology as to undermine the nature of the church? Does the individual replace the community as the center of reflection and life? Has the Pietist legacy aided and reflected an accent on singular pronouns which has little in common with the corporate consciousness of the biblical milieu?

In their attitude toward the church, Spener, Francke, and their early followers felt themselves to be loyal. In sermons, letters, and writings, Spener repeatedly professed to be a *rechtgläubig* ("orthodox") Lutheran in complete agreement with the teachings of the church and the Formula of Concord "in all articles and points."[2] Paul Grünberg, Spener's foremost biographer who authored three volumes about the father of Pietism, felt that one does not correctly understand Spener without recognizing that all his critical, subjectivizing, skeptical, and moralizing tendencies could not destroy the kernel of his churchly orthodoxy.[3] Whether or not he succeeded, Spener aspired to be looked upon as a faithful servant of the church. He was not so regarded by many of his opponents. Pietism was charged with subversive individualism and fundamental deviations in respect to the dogma and creeds of the church. The apologists for Pietism countered by asserting that it was the so-called "orthodox" and not they who were guilty of a basic departure from Luther in the form of degenerate Scholasticism. In spite of these protestations of true Lutheranism on both sides, a fundamental cleavage evolved between later Lutheran Orthodoxy and German Pietism. This became most evident in attitudes toward soteriology, dogma and creeds, the sacraments, and practical reforms.

Regeneration

Basic ecclesiological differences can be seen in the shift of emphasis in Pietism from justification to regeneration. Pietist scholars such as Martin Schmidt designate *Wiedergeburt* ("the new birth") as the underlying motif of Pietistic theology. It is said that this biological metaphor occupied for Spener and his followers the place which the juridical metaphor of justification occupied for Luther and the other mainline Reformers.

Schmidt likewise judges that the centrality of the doctrine of regeneration, rather than the establishment of conventicles, is most responsible for the swing from churchly consciousness to private edification. He believes that in Pietism is found a shift in emphasis from the Head of the church to the members of the church, from the development of the body to the edification of the new or inner man.[4] Since the new man is the goal of all church activity, the kingdom is equated, according to this interpretation, with two concepts basic to Pietism, *Erbauung* ("edification") and *Gottseligkeit* ("godliness"). The condition of the church is then judged by the members' experience and health rather than by their relationship to the Head. A fruitful life is more important than participation in the sacraments; individuals find unity in life rather than in Christ. This is the theological framework which led to the individualistic view of the church as a union of pious individuals or an aggregate of saved souls.

Although such a critique of Pietism contains much truth, especially in analyzing later manifestations, it is not fair to Spener's position. Spener felt that the Johannine and Pauline metaphor of regeneration represented a completion and an enhancement rather than a replacement of the equally biblical metaphor of justification. One can argue that Luther's use of personal pronouns to explicate the doctrine of justification was as influential as the Pietists' personalization of regeneration in abetting individualism. Similarly, one can claim that Spener felt community is needed as much as a vehicle for God's power to change persons as for power to forgive sinners. Moreover, Spener defined the inner man in order to encompass rather than eliminate the need for community. In the *Pia Desideria* he equated "inward" with "awakening love of God and neighbor through suitable means."[5] According to him, regeneration results from the activity of God primarily through the church; the fruitful life is life in Christ; and the new man's godliness is intended to reform the church. We may conclude our study of this doctrine with what may become a theme in reference to other issues: Spener and his followers opened the door for many manifestations of Protestant individualism; nevertheless, they did attempt to maintain a balance between their understanding of God's objective activity in Word and Sacrament and their stress on the individual and corporate human appropriation of Word and Sacrament.

Church Dogma and Creeds

Through a look at the Pietist's general attitude toward official dogma, we can more clearly understand the Pietist stance toward the church. Rather than repudiating doctrine as ineffective for life, the Pietists felt that there should be a reformation of both doctrine and life. On many occasions Spener agreed with his orthodox colleagues concerning the necessity of fixed doctrinal forms and the insufficiency of the good life without correct belief. But he joined with others in reacting against some of the views of Lutheran Scholasticism in which Luther's use of "pure" in referring to doctrine had been transferred to apply to the church itself. Because the church possessed pure doctrine, it was considered infallible. John Mayer, one of Spener's chief opponents, was outraged because Spener did not believe the evangelical church to be without error.[6] Not only the church, but Luther himself was elevated, being hailed by some as the thirteenth disciple. The

Symbolical Books had become invested with divine inspiration. Schelwig, another opponent, called Spener "sectarian" for asserting that the church needs reformation. For "it is not the Church but the ungodly in the Church that must be reformed."[7] This extreme position led to the Pietist countercharges of "Romanism." Since the possession of dogmatic infallibility was claimed by academic faculties and clerical bodies, Spener observed that one pope would be better than many popes.[8] In rejecting the identification of the kingdom and the church, Pietism was guilty of subjective tendencies in the same way as the major Protestant reformers, who had proclaimed that the judgment of God falls even upon the church. If the Protestant principle embodies "the rejection of every human claim to finality and absoluteness" in the name of the transcendent God,[9] the earliest Pietists manifested it in many ways more consistently than their opponents.

But this principle has frequently resulted in private dogmatism. God's transcendence is unconsciously rejected in the naive equalization of church doctrine with personal religious conviction. How far did Spener and Francke move in this direction? Reacting to the orthodoxy of their day, they made certain distinctions which are pertinent in discerning the degree of individualization in their emphasis. The first was Spener's distinction between esoteric and exoteric church dogma.

Esoteric and Exoteric

In light of the bitter polemics of his day, Spener thought it was best to hold some opinions privately and not expose them for public consideration.[10] He did not feel he contradicted basic church doctrine, but he did fear the unnecessary misunderstanding, bitterness, and controversy which might result from the frank exposé of all his private views. He desired nothing more than to appear in public to be thoroughly orthodox. Few could find fault with the basic Lutheranism of his catechism, which he published partially to give evidence of his doctrinal soundness.[11] He believed that in public pronouncements one should use customary doctrinal modes of speaking because of suspicions which might be engendered by the new and different.

Spener's admonitions to his followers concerning excessive mention of doctrine were motivated not so much out of fear of heterodoxy as out of concern for public relations. For example, he counseled a friend not to make mention of his views about "the inner speaking of God with the soul," for those pearls should "not be thrown before swine, which step on them and seek to tear us apart because of them."[12] The nature of this friend's opinion suggests that Spener privately approved views which were suspect by his contemporaries, including some esoteric opinions of exorcism, mysticism, and the Lord's Supper. We know about these through his private letters, in which he shared more freely and which he only reluctantly allowed to be published late in his career. Spener's distinction between esoteric and exoteric dogma may witness to a churchmanship, which placed the peace and welfare of the total church above the right to bring every personal notion to review. On the other hand, this distinction may have embodied attributes of theological double-talk. It did, however, open the door to the exaltation of the individual religious opinion over the traditional and collective witness of the church.

Primary and Secondary

The division of dogma into esoteric and exoteric was made less hypocritical and more logical by Spener's distinction between primary and secondary matters of belief. In this the first Pietists were correctly judged to be the inheritors of the Calixtine appeal to reduce dogma to essentials and not require conformity in nonessentials. According to Spener, there were important things about which one could not remain neutral.[13] A greater spirit of freedom, tolerance, and private opinion was permissible only in matters of secondary importance. Spener and Francke vigorously denied the accusations of dogmatic indifference. They merely regarded the detailed edifice woven by the subtleties and sophistry of Protestant Scholasticism as unimportant and even damaging. In contradistinction to this maze, they repeatedly spoke of *"alte Simplizität"* (apostolic simplicity), with which they could present the entire contents of the Christian faith in less than an hour. Luther, they felt, had it; Spener wanted to bring it back. Whereas Calixtus (the humanistic and ecumenical theologian of the early seventeenth century) had reduced the essentials to the Apostles' Creed, Spener engaged in a bold attempt to state precisely "the basic doctrines on which our salvation and faith depends, which are positively necessary."[14] Two doctrines are of the greatest importance: acknowledgment of our unholiness and incapacity; and faith in Christ the Son of God, who is true man, who has made satisfaction for us, who has gained for us forgiveness and reconciliation, and who has given power and impulses to our new life, of which he is the norm and rule. Or more simply, "The ground of our entire faith is Jesus Christ, who for us was made by God wisdom, righteousness, sanctification, and redemption."[15] According to Spener, instead of attempting to bring an unbeliever to articles of faith through philosophical science, it is far better to bring him personally to see the merits and power of Christ. From this central point, the Holy Spirit will enlighten him further concerning doctrine.

Religious Freedom

An interesting by-product of the desire for simplicity was the impetus for a spirit of tolerance and religious freedom. In unimportant matters Spener coveted not only the right of withholding judgment in disputed questions but also a certain latitude in determining his own theological convictions. What he sought for himself, he believed, should be extended to others. Spener reasoned that the limitations of theological knowledge which result from our finitude and human weakness make such freedom necessary. Whatever is beyond basic doctrine, therefore, belongs to the area of human freedom — freedom which will prevent any papal-like ruling over conscience. God, in his own time, will bring judgment on error. Moreover, history teaches that unanimity in secondary questions can never be attained.[16] As a result, when Spener found orthodoxy in the foundation of faith, he could look with patience and compassion on grievous errors in more secondary matters. Of necessity, true faith exists alongside existing errors. The mass conversions in the book of Acts provide a case in point, for it is certain, he reasoned, that some errant opinions remained with many of these new Christians for a long time.[17]

Early Pietism, however, did not only grant tolerance in matters which were considered nonessentials; the principle of religious freedom was also applied to fundamentals. Although Spener and Francke labored for stricter disciplinary measures within the church, they opposed the coercive hand of the state in religious affairs. They taught that heresy should be fought vigorously — with the weapons of prayer for unbelievers, love for heretics, persuasion instead of physical force, and argumentation by pious example. Their position was summarized in the popular Latin saying: *in necessarii veritas (unitas), in non necessarii libertas, in omnibus caritas* ("in necessary things, truth (or unity), in things not necessary, liberty, in all things, love").[18] This plea for tolerance and religious freedom combined with the indifference and rationalism of the Enlightenment to lead to greater subjectivism. Nevertheless, Spener, Francke, and their colleagues desired to walk the middle ground between dogmatic inflexibility and dogmatic indifference.

Symbolical Books

Illustrative of these general attitudes to church dogma was Pietism's view of the Symbolical Books. Spener defined Pietists as "those who honor *symbolische Bücher.*"[19] It is true that Pietistic motifs can be found extensively in the Symbolical Books. Nevertheless, a fundamental cleavage developed between Pietism and its orthodox opponents in the overall evaluation of these documents. In contrast to his orthodox contemporaries, who elevated the documents nearly to the level of Scripture, Spener, who was a competent church and secular historian, applied the tools of higher criticism to them. According to Spener, the example of the apostolic church demonstrates that Symbolical Books are not absolutely essential to faith. It would in fact have been better if the church could have avoided the disputes which made the Formula of Concord necessary, but given the circumstances, we should be very thankful for the Formula's clarifications. Spener said the Symbolical Books are of human origin, and while God has provided so that they would not contain errors in basic doctrines which are necessary for salvation, He did permit errors in secondary matters to remind us of the distinction between the Symbolical Books and the Holy Scriptures. By this historical approach, Spener no doubt helped to undermine faith in the verbal infallibility of the symbols.

How, then, did Pietism evaluate the usefulness and authority of these creedal statements for its own day? Both Spener and Francke said creedal statements are worthwhile because they provide a "rule of doctrine" and "a bond and evidence of unity." They claimed that in doctrinal disputes the church has the power and the right to decide what to accept and what to condemn as obligatory standards for its teachers and servants.[20] After declaring such allegiance, however, these Pietist leaders proceeded to qualify their acceptance. They proclaimed that creedal statements possess authority only inasmuch as they meet scriptural tests. Unlike their opponents, who would not accept any doctrinal deductions from Scripture which were not in the creedal formulations of the church, the

Pietists did not feel limited to the Symbolical Books. Nor did they feel obliged to accept any extensions or implications of the Symbolical Books which were formulated by theologians and faculties.

According to Spener, it was not necessary for laymen to be articulate concerning the Symbolical Books: only teachers and clergy should be required to subscribe to them. One who could not come to such agreement had two alternatives. If he or she could prove an error in the Symbolical Books, Spener maintained, the church should then remove this error. If that was impossible and the person still had qualms about the doctrine, then Spener knew no other counsel than to have the person leave the church or, on less important issues, pledge silence.

Here we note the tension in Spener's thought between the interest, welfare, and authority of the church on the one side and the freedom of conscience bound only to Scripture and personal convictions on the other. Spener himself never had to face the consequences of this tension because he agreed with the substance of the Symbolical Books and the Bible, but he did deal a powerful blow to the authority of the symbols and their compulsory nature for the individual. As a result, the overall attitude of the Pietist leaders concerning the creeds was responsible not only for a reduction in the number of doctrines but also for a change in the basic evaluation of those doctrines.

Visible and Invisible Church

These changes in doctrine led to a revised doctrine of the church, as can be seen in the beliefs concerning the visible and invisible church. Since the first Pietists regarded themselves to be of one mind with Luther, they believed that the invisible church consists of the multitude of all true children of God while the visible church (in this case Lutheran) is a part of the invisible church which teaches true doctrine and administers the sacraments correctly. In spite of this alleged agreement, Pietism tended to shift its stress from the visible to the invisible church. Spener and Francke did not go as far as many Radical Pietists like Gottfried Arnold, who characterized his historical writing as *unparteyisch*, meaning that his view was not attached to any confession but intent on the true invisible church. Spener, however, did approach this spiritualistic view in his distinction between true heart religion and Lutheran formalism, as did Francke in his differentiation between the converted and unconverted.

So long as the redeemed, converted, regenerated, or pious were unidentifiable, these Pietist beliefs led toward the invisible church — the true church in the midst of the actual, visible church. But as soon as it was felt that such people could be identified by outward marks, this stress on the invisible was transformed into a definition of the visible as something other than just the Lutheran church of that day. For this reason early Pietism was accused of the Anabaptist error of equating the true invisible church with a separate visible community. In theory both Spener and Francke denied such charges; in practice Francke, with his greater stress on the experiential aspects of conversion, was instrumental in leading Pietism in this direction.

Another characteristic of early Pietism which led to a greater accent on the invisible church was the more irenic and tolerant attitude toward those from other traditions such as the Reformed, the Eastern Orthodox, and, in individual cases, even Roman Catholics.[21] All of these tendencies, however, must be viewed in the light of Spener and Francke's churchmanship and great loyalty to their own Lutheran church. They attempted to take mystical and spiritualistic motifs, which tend to be destructive of the visible church, and make them fruitful for their own institutional life. As a result they have been given credit for bequeathing a churchly impulse to later movements such as Romanticism, the Enlightenment, and German Idealism. Their stress on the invisible, which was a reaction to the near apotheosis of the visible church, inevitably led to a degree of subjectivization of church doctrine. How far the Pietists moved in this direction is a question which is difficult to resolve.

Sacraments

Pietism's stance toward the sacraments followed a pattern which was consistent with its overall doctrinal posture. Affirming that their theological position was identical with that of Luther and the primitive church, the early Pietists claimed they did not want to deviate from the means of grace and the orthodox position regarding them. But they felt that the view of later orthodoxy had degenerated into an *opus operatum*. They would have agreed with a later historian's comment that their opponents "assigned an efficacy to priestly functions and to sacraments which involved a species of deism, a substitution of the second cause for the first as thoroughgoing as is implied in any of the postulated claims of Romanism."[22] Their opponents, on the other hand, accused them of adopting a mystical and spiritualistic interpretation of the sacraments. Spener, as customary, desired to walk the middle ground: "As in all things, two extremes are possible. It is a deviation to place your trust outwardly in the mere custom of the sacrament and be concerned little with the inward. But it is also a deviation when one chooses to despise and set aside the outward because of the inward."[23] According to Spener, God deals with us through outward means as long as we live in the flesh. Therefore, the spiritual man who holds fast to the simple Word of God desires in no way to take away from the outward ordinances. How, then, were these general principles applied to baptism, the Lord's Supper, and the confessional?

Baptism

Spener and Francke were quite orthodox in their views on baptism. All grounds for confident faith and all impulses toward Christian living rest on baptism. Our subsequent repentance and faith are a putting on of baptism; in fact, Christianity is merely the practice of baptism. Spener and Francke defended infant baptism with all of the traditional arguments. In this they held to the objective efficacy of the sacrament. Spener wrote, "Therefore I do not even know how to praise baptism and its power highly enough, and I believe it is the true bath of regeneration and is the renewal of the Holy Spirit."[24]

Inherent in their definitions, however, are deviations significant to this study. Because of their emphasis on the subjective appropriation of salvation through faith and repentance, the early Pietists opposed any conception of infant baptism which smacked of *opus operatum*. For this reason, Spener raised serious questions concerning the practice of exorcism (driving out demons through refutation by words) in relation to infant baptism. He failed to clarify his position, however, since he regarded this as a secondary matter and preferred to remain esoteric, feeling that open discussion might cause more harm than good. One of Spener's most radical departures was his exclusion not only of unbaptized Christian children but also of Jewish and Turkish children from the damnation of original sin because, he maintained, the article on original sin declares only the consequences of sin and does not explain what God's mercy can effect outside the general ordinance.[25] Likewise, Spener's stress on the possibility of losing the new birth following baptism and on the new obedience which baptism requires significantly altered traditional baptism.

These deviations, which resulted from the emphasis on repentance, conversion, and regeneration and which were held in conjunction with a purely orthodox view of infant baptism, produced a tension in early Pietism which was never fully resolved by either Spener or Francke. They did sense the problem, however, and occasionally touched upon it. The incongruity of lamenting the number of unregenerate preachers while at the same time theorizing that those same preachers had received baptismal new birth was partially resolved by maintaining that it is possible to fall from baptismal grace. Apostasy is not inevitable, however, because of the possibility of continual growth in grace.

The belief that salvation is a process helped to resolve the problem resulting from the impossibility of an infant participating in the subjective appropriation of salvation demanded by the early Pietists. For this reason both Spener and Francke placed great emphasis on catechetical instruction and public confirmation. While in Dresden, Spener expressed his desire that confirmation be public as it had been in Frankfurt in order that "the promises which had been made at the time of baptism by the godfather might be vividly remembered and at this time be confessed orally by the person himself."[26] The Pietists' need for subjective appropriation made it possible for some of the followers of Spener and Francke to minimize infant baptism in favor of the later conversion experience and to circumvent the objective efficacy of the sacrament. Francke and Spener, however, attempted to avoid this tendency.

The Lord's Supper

With respect to the Lord's Supper, the early Pietists again professed to be traditionally Lutheran. Contrary to the charge that they spiritualized it and made it merely a memorial meal, both early leaders emphasized that in the Lord's Supper we enjoy the true natural body of Christ. Since he followed Luther in his distaste for philosophy, Spener did not attempt to define in detail the exact nature of the real bodily presence. Instead he insisted that even though we cannot understand, we must trust God's truth, or we rely on his Word in vain. He judged the Reformed tradition to be guilty of natural reason which rejects the omnipresence of Christ; for according to the Reformed conception of the purely spiritual benefits of Communion, one would receive through the sacrament no more than he could enjoy through faith alone. "It is certain that the mature Christian remembers and proclaims the death of Christ apart from the Lord's Supper."[27] But the sacrament does not stand or fall on the believer's act of remembrance; the Lord instituted it in order to participate in it by his presence in the bread and wine. Charges of moralism were countered by holding strongly to the admittance of the unworthy to the Lord's Supper. To do otherwise, according to Spener, would weaken the doctrine of the true presence. Christ gave his life and shed his blood for all.

Confession

The *Beichtstuhl* ("confessional") figured prominently in Pietist controversies. Although it was practically considered a sacrament by many of the orthodox, Spener and Francke felt freer to attack it than the two traditional Protestant sacraments. This was due in part to the great latitude in German Lutheranism itself. Western and southern Germany knew nothing of the compulsory nature of this ordinance which arose anew in middle and northern Germany following the Reformation. Spener's views stemmed from his orientation at Strasbourg, where believers had opportunity, without compulsion or fees, for confession before partaking of the Lord's Supper. Spener deplored the supplementary income received by ministers who heard confessions; to him this was an abuse of the confessional.[28] One of Francke's first innovations at Glaucha was his refusal to accept money for this service.

More basically, their objections stemmed from their subjective reaction to the mechanization, impersonality in administration, and *opus operatum* view they observed in many churches. Compulsory confession had combined with oversized parishes to make impossible an effective ministration on the part of the pastor. As a result, parishioners frequently stood in long lines to participate en masse in a service in which they all received absolution at the same time. Spener protested this perfunctory treatment, which tended to identify the words of the confessor with God's forgiveness and to bypass repentance as a concomitance of absolution. "Because God has joined together repentance and forgiveness, no man is able to separate the same."[29]

But the Pietists were not entirely negative in their critique; they did advocate some positive revisions. Spener himself could never quite call for the abolition of the confessional. Instead, he favored its proper use in an intimate and personal relationship between pastor and people or between enlightened Christians. He favored the practice used successfully by Francke at Glaucha. Following a general service in which Francke gave admonitions to all, individuals were free either to accept or reject private confession. Francke's usage became incorporated in an order by Friedrich III which also stipulated that a person had to register eight days before the service of confession.[30] Francke himself confessed to a neighboring minister four times each year before partaking of the Lord's Supper. In spite of these efforts at reform, it is very likely that Pietism, with its critical stance and opposition to compulsion, abetted the demise of the confessional. By its insistence on the close relationship of repentance and forgiveness, the subjective side of the Divine-human encounter was accentuated.

Practical Reforms

The need, desire, and effort for a new reformation of the church constituted the major concern of Pietism. Spener defined a Pietist as "a person who uses all his energy to improve the church."[31] There had already been a reformation of doctrine. But instead of building upon this pure foundation, the church had experienced stagnation, even retrogression, acquiescing to pure doctrine without allowing the fruits of piety to follow. Spener issued a clarion call for reformation in the opening statements of his *Pia Desideria*:

> Let us therefore be diligent in investigating even more deeply our own shortcomings and those of the rest of the church in order that we may learn to know our sicknesses, and then with a fervent invocation of God for the light of his Spirit let us also search for and ponder over the remedies. . . . What is impossible for men remains possible for God. Eventually God's hour must come, if only we wait for it.[32]

This expectation of better times for the church was defined in terms of restitutionism — restoring the pattern of the primitive church. What was possible then, Spener asserted, is not impossible today. The Holy Spirit, which has been sent to us by God, is still just as powerful and willing to accomplish his work of sanctification in us.

Implicit in any program of reformation is a thorough criticism of the existing church, and Spener and Francke felt free to criticize nearly everything about their own

church except its doctrine. Such an attitude, when encountered by opposition, frequently leads to despair and
disparagement instead of reform. This is what happened
with Radical Pietists such as Arnold, Hoburg, Petersen,
Breckling, and Dippel. To them the church became Babel,
the great whore Babylon of the apocalypse; the hated
ministry was identified with the wicked kings. Spener and
Francke refused to go this far. In *Laments over Corrupted
Christendom*, Spener defended the duty of complaining
against the abuses in the church but denied that the Lutheran Church was Babel or that any member was en-
titled to abstain from communion or services.[33] He defined
Pietists as those who work with patience in the same fellowship in order to bring the church and those who err
back to the Word of God and the sacraments. These twin
themes of judgment and reform, when applied to the
practical side of the life of the church, bequeathed to Pietism both its strengths and weaknesses, for the zealous
ideas of reform of the first generation easily took different
shapes with the second. Consequently, both values and
dangers can be observed in their practical reform proposals for a regenerate clergy, a practiced priesthood of all
believers, a revised polity, and the formation of small
groups as a means to achieve all of these.

A Regenerate Clergy

Spener and Francke regarded the reform of the clergy
as integral to any program of reformation of the church as
a whole. In contradistinction to those who believed that
the church would be in the best condition possible only
if it were rid of the dangers presented by the proponents

of the false religious faiths, Spener discerned that the trouble lay within, beginning with the clergy themselves. "There is no doubt in my mind that we would soon have a completely transformed church if we teachers, or at least a majority of us, were able without embarrassment to call on our congregations as Paul did in I Cor. 11:1: 'Be imitators of me as I am of Christ.' "[34] The Pietists opposed the rationalization for the low state of morality of a large segment of the clergy which arose as a result of the exclusive emphasis on the office instead of on the man. Likewise, there was a reaction to the conditions faced by John Winckler of Hamburg. With some thirty thousand persons whom he did not know personally, he wondered whether he could really be a pastor. The Leipzig theological faculty offered reassurance from the example of the prophet Jonah, who ministered effectively to many times the number of Winckler's parishioners: "Who will believe that Jonah undertook special and individual care of each of his hearers?"[35]

In opposition to this attitude the early Pietists proposed a remedial program consisting of personal relationships with parishioners, pastoral visitation, Bible classes, and prayer meetings. The pastor should be a shepherd of souls, not a mere official, and his means should not be coercion but the example of his pure and holy life. Students were to be trained accordingly. Preachers were urged to adopt a plain and simple style of preaching. In reviving this emphasis on the righteousness of the clergy, were Spener and Francke guilty of the Donatist heresy? Were they responsible for modifying the image of the minister from that of preacher of the Word to that of example?

Certain statements by Spener and Francke seemed to justify the frequent charge of Donatism by their opponents. Francke wrote that a preacher must first love Christ. His own heart must be warmed or his discourses "will be apt to be cold and lifeless, and therefore unprofitable and fruitless."[36] He desired courage for the many who were fearful that if they criticized and exposed ungodly ministers they would be "accounted Donatists."[37] Nevertheless, Spener was careful not to dispute the efficacy of the ministry rendered by unspiritual preachers; he asserted only an essential lessening of their effectiveness.[38]

> It is not my intention to conclude from this that no good has been accomplished through such persons and their work, not that true faith and a true conversion may not have been brought about in somebody through them, for the Word does not receive its divine power from the person of the one who proclaims it but has this power in itself.[39]

Spener remained faithful to the classical Protestant doctrine of justification by faith alone while at the same time stressing the moral requirements for the ministry proposed in I Timothy and Titus. Thus early Pietism desired the subjective appropriation of the fruits of the Spirit for the ministry while at the same time it denied the anthropomorphic roots for these fruits.

Priesthood of All Believers

According to the Pietists, the church needed more than a regenerate clergy if the desired reforms were to be carried out. They called for a greater manifestation of

Luther's basic doctrine of the priesthood of all believers. Alluding to this motif throughout *Pia Desideria,* Spener clarified it further in *Spiritual Priesthood,* where he defined spiritual priesthood as "the right which our Saviour Jesus Christ has purchased for all men, and for which He anoints all believers with His Holy Spirit, in virtue of which they may and shall bring sacrifices acceptable to God, pray for themselves and others, and severally edify themselves and their neighbors."[40] In this way every Christian possesses a triple ministry of sacrifice, prayer, and edification through the Word. The first involves yielding all — body and soul, property and passions — to the Redeemer. The second consists of intercession for Christian brothers and sisters. By the third all are required to exhort and console one another.[41]

In the spirit of this position early Pietism worked to eliminate the great chasm which separated clergy and laity. Spener asserted that the name "priest" is a general name for all Christians and applies to ministers no differently than to other Christians. Francke's references to the differences between laity and clergy were expressed even more strongly: "What horrid Mischief this wicked distinction is the cause of. . . ."[42] Both of these leaders, however, avoided a Quaker stance and maintained a functional distinction between clergy and laity. Spener held that a special call is required if one is to exercise publicly the office of ministry, but such a call should enhance and not hinder the exercise of the general spiritual priesthood. Specifically, lay people might perform baptism, but they should not be allowed to consecrate the Eucharist.[43]

Spener felt, as on so many other issues, that he was in

complete agreement with Luther's proposition that general priesthood is the treasure of the entire church. For Luther, however, the spiritual priesthood was not one in which each believer acquired direct access to God apart from the ministry and sacraments of the church. Instead, the priesthood constituted a service in which each believer is a Christ or a priest to his or her neighbor. For the most part, Spener and Francke were consistently Lutheran; nevertheless, they and their followers often stretched Luther's definitions in their appeal for a more democratic church polity and in the mystical tendencies inherent in the style of the conventicles.

A More Democratized Polity

The Lutheran church of Spener's day was characterized by rigid class distinctions. There were three classes — the princely, the priestly, and the lay — and each class knew its own definite sphere of activity. For example, it was disreputable for an aristocratic child to be baptized in the same water as a common child. Pietism represented a reaction against the extremities of these distinctions. Spener was criticized for the egalitarianism of his pastoral service and his small group meetings, in which servants were allowed to sit at the same tables as their masters. The more radical Gottfried Arnold agreed with Spener's actions: "The miserable child of a beggar . . . is just as valuable in God's sight as a prince."[44]

To the first estate, the civil rulers, Spener granted the God-given duty of enforcing the first as well as the second table of the law. Yet he deplored the prevalent corruption:

. . . how few there are who remember that God gave them

their scepters and staffs in order that they use their power to advance the kingdom of God! Instead, most of them, as is customary with great lords, live in those sins and debaucheries which usually go along with court life and are regarded as virtually inseparable from it, while other magistrates are intent on seeking their own advantage.[45]

Spener opposed what he termed an irresponsible caesaropapism.[46] The territorial princes used their power of appointment to promote their own purposes. In the consistories, the secular powers combined with the clergy to so dominate church life as to rule out the third estate. Consequently, Spener believed that churches living under authorities of a different faith are in a better position: they at least have the advantage of being able to manage their own affairs.[47] And if persecution comes, they might share in the glorious condition of the early church, which was at its best in times of duress.

Though Spener desired increased participation by the common people, he did not intend to eliminate entirely the authority of the secular and clerical rulers. His program included the reformation of all three estates. He believed that all members should assume responsibility in the affairs of the church. Congregations should be divided into groups under lay presidents. His desire for such a board of elders is indicative of his presbyterian bias in polity, which may be traced to his matriculation at Strasbourg and Geneva. Congregations should participate in selecting their own pastors. Laity and ministers both should be included in synods. Francke shared with Spener the conviction that the elders of each congregation should join the pastor in disciplining the congregation, a practice which they admired in Calvinistic churches.

Pietism contributed to the church an increased democratization of polity. For some this is synonymous with subjectivization of doctrine; for others democratic polity does not preclude the objective authority of the gospel. Spener and Francke expounded this emphasis for the reformation of the church and the more universal appropriation of its ministries on the part of individual Christians. They deplored the resultant autonomy of the individual which emerged in some Pietist circles.

Collegia Pietatis

Engendering the most criticism and accusations of subjectivism were the small group meetings known variously as *collegia pietatis,* conventicles, *ecclesiolae,* or *collegia philobiblica.* Although the Smalkald Articles had permitted mutual brotherly instruction from God's Word, Bucer in his later years at Strasbourg had instituted groups called Christian fellowships, and Jacob Boehme had participated in house meetings in Görlitz as early as 1600, all of these previous groups were so sparse and short-lived that Spener's small gatherings inaugurated a major innovation in the ecclesiastical life of his day. They evolved naturally from the success of his Sunday afternoon catechetical services, which were open to everyone. Parents were encouraged to help prepare their children for these exercises and consequently learned much themselves. Spener began to include in his morning sermons catechetical prefaces on which the gathering was examined in the afternoon.

In principle the *collegia pietatis* — the private gatherings which met on Mondays and Thursdays in Spener's home from 1670 to 1682 — were but an extension of the values derived from his catechetical activities. The nature of these gatherings can be discerned from the words of Spener himself:

> I either repeated in summary fashion the sermon held the previous Sunday or repeated from the New Testament a few verses . . . and then the men present discussed these things without contention or disquiet. . . . All the people had free access to these exercises, often as many as the place would hold, nevertheless the women were separated from the men so that the latter could not see them. The subject was at all times the text at hand. . . . Until 1682 the exercises were established in this way in my house but on advice of the city council and a special conference called by the rulers they were moved to the church, although to be truthful, not without detriment, in that some of the middle class who had often spoken something for their own and others' edification in the home, ceased to speak in such a public place and thus a certain part of the previous fruitfulness was lost.[48]

In addition to discussions concerning sermons and their texts, the gatherings came to include prayers, the reading of devotional literature, and the study of additional passages of Scripture.

In accordance with the original purpose, these conventicles were to supplement and not supplant the regular church services. The Lord's Supper was forbidden in the private gatherings. In spite of this and other safeguards, however, the conventicles soon gave rise to movements toward separation. One of the members at Frankfurt, a wealthy jurist named Johann Jakob Schütz, separated, and in 1682, the year when the gatherings were forced to meet in the church, another group withdrew. Some of these groups eventually emigrated to Pennsylvania, one group

led by Johann Kelpius in 1694. Spener was disturbed by all
separatist tendencies and attempted to persuade all to
return to the church. This was the purpose of his tract
*The Use and the Misuse of the Laments over Corrupted
Christendom,* which appeared in 1684 and was reprinted
in 1687 and 1696. In this tract Spener stated that even
though the church was corrupt, it was the true church
from which no one should turn away. By 1703, in spite of
the official approval of the *collegia pietatis* held in
churches, Spener had grown cautious. He seriously ques-
tioned the value of introducing such meetings and consequently established no conventicles in his own ministry
in either Dresden or Berlin. He repeatedly deplored sepa-
ration, "claiming that it acted like a medicine which was
more dangerous than the disease it was supposed to
cure."[49]

The centrality of the doctrine of regeneration; the doubt
concerning the finality of Scholastic formulations and the
Symbolical Books; the distinction between esoteric and
exoteric as well as primary and secondary in matters of
doctrine; the greater spirit of toleration toward other
communions; the emphasis on the subjective appropriation
of God's grace in the sacraments; and the program of
reformation through regenerate clergy, the priesthood of
all believers, a democratic polity, and *collegia pietatis* —
all contained individualistic tendencies. Nevertheless, the
extreme expression of self-assertion against external church
authority which more and more emancipated itself from
the restraints of tradition was the work of later Pietism.
It is true that Spener and Francke opened the door to such

individualism through their protest against the doctrinal rigidity of Scholasticism and the low state of morality present in church and culture. Overall, however, they desired application and not rejection of doctrine, participation in and not repudiation of church government, reformation of and not separation from the church.

III

Inner and Outer Word: The View of the Bible

Pietism exalted the supremacy of the Bible above all other external standards. Did this represent a return to the classical Protestant emphasis on the authority of the Word, or did it in reality lead to the perils of private interpretation? Pietism stressed the teleological application of the Scriptures in daily life. Did this shift to the practical lead to a pragmatism in which the Bible ultimately came to be tested by humanistic values? Pietism taught that true exegesis is the work of the internal testimony of the Holy Spirit. Did it view the Bible as the primary vehicle of the Spirit, or did this lead to a circumventing of Scripture by Spirit? Pietism believed that the regenerate could understand the Scriptures better than could the unregenerate. Did this imply that conversion must precede biblical study instead of being a result of it? Pietism abetted the rise of higher criticism. Is it to be blamed or is it to be praised for the impact of such hermeneutical endeavors on subsequent theology? These are the most important questions to be considered in an evaluation of the relative subjectivity of Pietism's view of the Bible.

Biblical Authority

Pietism joined the Puritan legacy in giving the Bible the central place which it has held in traditional Protestantism. Pietism definitely represented a back-to-the-Bible movement. From 1712 to 1812, the Halle-based Canstein Bible Institute (the first Bible Society) published more than two million Bibles and one million New Testaments. Even more than Spener, Francke is regarded as having placed the Bible at the center of Christian life. Paul Tillich observed that "wherever biblical theology prevails over systematic theology, that is almost always due to the influence of Pietism."[1] Exegesis came to the fore; dogmatics became simply an ordered summary of biblical theology.

Spener and Francke agreed with Lutheran orthodoxy that the Scriptures were the source and norm of correct doctrine. In a letter of 1688, Spener avowed the verbal inspiration of the Scriptures, and he repudiated all hypotheses which in any way encroached upon this certainty.[2] Nevertheless, he departed from the mechanical view of inspiration which was in vogue in Scholasticism. "We need not think that the Holy Spirit Himself or through an angel had to speak words to the writers or to dictate them, but He gave them divine truth through an inner enlightenment of the heart."[3]

It was in their exaltation of the Bible as the supreme authority over the claims of doctrinal interpreters and church symbols that the early Pietists differed most with their contemporaries. In discussing polity Francke concluded, "Thou shalt not be judged by any Church-Ordinance, but according to God's Word."[4] Spener advised lay members to "search the Scriptures, so that they may test the teaching of their preacher. . . . If they perceive ministers to be erroneous, they should guard themselves against such false teaching."[5] He professed agreement with Luther's declaration that Holy Scripture alone is the rule of faith and must be understood out of itself and not from the interpretations of the church, the fathers, councils, or teachers.

Illustrative of this general principle were Spener's prejudice concerning commentaries and his attitude toward the Symbolical Books. Though he did not teach that one should disparage the exegetical labors of others, he did feel that one should strive after an independent judgment and not acquiesce in a slavish use of commentaries. Consequently, he spoke against the proposal for a *glossierten* Bible because it might become normative, win the status of a symbol, and encroach upon the necessary freedom of exegetical study.[6] Similarly, he repeatedly asserted that the Symbolical Books are binding insofar as they agree with the Holy Scriptures. He felt that the creeds had undermined the science of exegesis because of the common practice of finding in the Bible only what was sanctioned by the Formula of Concord. As a corrective he proposed that one should search "to discover the will of God in the Bible rather than to prove the authority of a confession of faith. . . ."[7]

Such exaltation of the Bible above the Symbolical Books tended to undercut the authority of the church. The early Pietists believed their method was consistently Lutheran and that their great reverence for the Bible saved them from the perils of extreme individualism. Their opponents disagreed. They claimed that the Pietists only substituted private for churchly interpretation, and that by weakening the respect for ecclesiastical exegetes Pietism abetted the undermining of the authority of the Bible itself. The Pietists countered by arguing that the Bible would become alive only through freedom from rigid, dogmatic formulations. In the light of subsequent Protestant developments, however, Spener's belief that the study of the Bible alone would lead to dogmatic simplicity and unity proved to be somewhat naive. Exegetical study divorced from the counterbalance of creed or church can lead to private interpretation in which the individual tends to find in the Scriptures exactly (and only) what he wants to find. Although Spener and Francke sought to be true to the total message of the Bible and were influenced (more than they realized) by their nurture in the orthodox tradition, many of their followers imposed private interpretations on the Bible in such a way as to be guilty of the exaltation of the inner word above the written Word.

Exegetically, Spener and Francke differed from their contemporaries not only in their view of Scripture as the supreme authority in the church but also in their stress on the practical purposes and goals of Bible study. They were closest to the orthodox in their theory of inspiration; they were furthest in the area of teleology. Their objective views coincided more than their subjective applications. Pietists believed the Bible had been communicated to man in order to edify, console, encourage, warn, reprimand, and help the church and its members as well as to lead men and women to God by bringing about repentance and

change. For Pietists the Bible became a devotional re-
source rather than a source of doctrine, a guide to life
rather than just the source of belief and faith. Spener
desired "Das Wort Gottes reichlich unter uns zu bringen"
("to bring abundantly the Word of God among us").[8]
"Since the Letter is examined only for the sake of the
Spirit of the Sacred Oracles, we should condemn whatever
cannot be reduced to some useful purpose. . . ."[9] His conception of the power and his concern for the efficacy of
the Holy Scriptures were eminently practical.

Was this emphasis an outgrowth of Biblical authority?
Or was it instead the basis for external criteria by which
the Bible was to be tested? Spener, Francke, and their sup-
porters asserted that these practical interests were but an
application of the demands inherent in the Scriptures.
Their opponents maintained that this teleological emphasis
shifted attention entirely from the experienced object to
the experiencing subject. In attempting any synthesis of
the opposing viewpoints, one must be fair to the intentions
of Spener and Francke while at the same time recognizing
that their practical views opened the door to later subjectivization which undermined the authority of the Bible
itself. How far they moved in this direction can be further
clarified by examining their views concerning the relationship between the Spirit and the Bible.

Internal Testimony of the Spirit

In his work against Pietism, Ludwig Fischlin, one of the
foremost early polemicists, attributed to Spener and his
followers the opinion that "the Holy Scripture is merely

a dead bookpiece and a mere outward signpost to Christ. . . ."[10] Though likely taken out of context, it is easy to see how such a statement could be deduced from Pietist reactions to the mechanization and materialization through which the Bible was viewed as a deposit of revelation finished and strongly efficacious in itself, detached from the living concerns and workings of the Holy Spirit. Spener felt that such an attitude correctly regarded the Holy Scriptures as the vehicle of faith but had forgotten the power of faith. Concerning the source of this power, Pietists alluded frequently to the *testimonium spiritus internum* ("internal testimony of the Spirit"), believing it is the Holy Spirit which enables the dead letter of the sacred writings to become a living power within us and which enlightens the mind of the believer in understanding. Spener spoke of "true faith which is awakened through the Word of God by the illumination, witness, and sealing of the Holy Spirit."[11] Francke's definition went even further:

> God, in his infinite mercy to his children, imparts to them the internal operation of his Spirit, at other seasons than when engaged in reading his Word. As he blesses the seed sown in the earth, and causes it to strike root, to flourish, and to bear abundant fruit; so does he incessantly nourish the incorruptible seed of his Word, with the richest outpourings of his grace.[12]

Francke's reference to "other seasons" raised the fundamental problem of determining the relationship of the Spirit to the Bible. Pietism's opponents feared that if the Holy Spirit was not bound to the Scriptures the objective validity, power, and meaning of the written Word would be destroyed. Spener agreed that proper knowledge and preaching of the Word is not dependent upon any special disposition of the heart, but he also believed that the written Word of God carries life in itself like a grain of seed. This inherent living power comes to life just as in a seed. And as the life cannot survive apart from the husk, so the Word and the Spirit cannot be separated. According to Spener, this was the mistake of both the Quakers on the one side and his opponents on the other.

Quakers tended to emphasize the Spirit to the detriment of the Bible. Although Spener felt it was unfortunate that it had come to the point that any mention of the Holy Spirit was immediately taken as Quakerism or Weigelianism, he did agree with the usual critiques of early Quakerism. Churchly Pietism as represented by Spener and Francke was far from the spiritualization of Jacob Boehme, who said, "Liegt doch die ganze Bibel in mir" ("the entire Bible lies in me").

While Spener believed that the Quakers exalted the Spirit at the expense of the Bible, he judged that his opponents had so apotheosized the written Word that they neglected the Holy Spirit. He feared that a Spiritless Scripture would paralyze the very religious life and aspirations which the Bible had been given to awaken. He charged that the very academicians who so strongly asserted that one should not separate Spirit from Word were guilty of doing so in their own lives.

To Spener the Bible was authoritarian, but the incessant working of the Holy Spirit was also a necessity. He desired to bring these together in a living relationship with the affirmation that the Holy Spirit does not work without the Bible or outside the Bible but in the Bible and through the Bible.[13] The Holy Spirit does not operate apart from means, and the means it utilizes is the Word. Though Pietism does insist upon direct communion with God through the Holy Spirit, such is not a communion to be brought about without the means of the Word.

Nevertheless, critics have insisted that Pietists frequently have emphasized the witness of the Spirit at the expense of scriptural authority. Martin Schmidt believes Spener was spiritualistic in his special emphasis which many times distinguished the Holy Spirit from the Word.[14] Such judgments are deduced from the many instances in which it is apparent that both Spener and Francke allowed the possibility of direct special revelations apart from the Bible. From the perspective of the Pietists, however, all such revelations were required to conform to Scripture. The Bible must at all times remain the norm in interpreting the content. Professor Nagler, the author of *Pietism and Methodism,* has compared Spener's position to that of Wesley, who felt that when the witness of the inner testimony of the Spirit went beyond God's standing testimony in Scripture, the inner testimony "was to be tested by Scripture."[15] Instead of allowing mystical experiences to undermine the authority of the canon as their opponents feared, the Pietists looked upon Biblical study as a real source of experience. They were convinced that the application of the Biblical test to all revelations guarded sufficiently against undesirable subjective tendencies. Their opponents, however, felt that any admission of special revelations opened the door to heretical spirtualism.

This accusation was especially apropos to the Donatist-like way in which Spener and Francke often made the efficacy and understanding of Scripture dependent upon the religious and moral dispositions of its scholars and preachers. Spener reasoned that the Holy Spirit does not work automatically in the Scriptures but instead becomes effective only under certain conditions. Scripture is in itself true and powerful, but it only becomes so for the individual who lets the Spirit rule by beginning Biblical exegesis with prayer, meditating on God's truth, and attempting to lead a holy life. Consequently, Spener inferred that only the regenerate can understand spiritual matters; the external sense of the Scriptures can be apprehended in a natural way, but the deep internal meaning can only be understood with the aid of the Spirit, who enlightens the mind.

Francke developed this more explicitly. He spoke of the literal sense which "ought then to be carefully distinguished from that sense which no one can apprehend, unless divinely illuminated by the Spirit who speaks in the Scriptures." The natural man does not perceive the things of the Spirit of God. Christ declared that the world cannot receive the Spirit of truth. St. Paul also affirmed that spiritual things are spiritually discerned. Francke bolstered such evidence with a quote from Melanchthon: "The gift of interpretation, indeed belongs not to the ungodly, but is with that assembly which is governed and sanctified by the Holy Spirit." And according to Augustine: "In the Scriptures, our eyes see with more or less clearness, according as we die more or less to the present world. . . ."[16] Francke probably moved to an extreme in his attempt to demonstrate the inability of the carnal mind to discern the sense of the letter of Scripture. This is indicative of the somewhat more radical and subjective nature of Francke's stance in comparison to that of Spener.

The basic issue revolves around the question of how the Bible can be the mediator of God's grace if the carnal mind cannot understand it. Does not this imply that salvation would of necessity be effected outside the Bible? Although Francke seems to imbibe the Donatist position to a greater extent than Spener, both would recoil from a moralism which implies that the efficacy of Scripture is altogether dependent upon the moral condition of the reader. The total context of their theology would stress that the Spirit, through the Word, changes the carnal to the spiritual to make understanding possible for all. The Bible remains the fundamental means of the Spirit. At many points, the overall position of Pietism approaches the existentialist stress on the priority of faith, the prerequisite to understanding.

Exegetical Implications

Pietism's view of the authority of the Bible and of the necessity of the inner testimony of the Holy Spirit nurtured significant practical exegetical implications which were to lead to greater freedom and subjectivity in hermeneutical science. Pietism represented a revival of the reading and study of the Bible for all and a new impetus to biblical theology among the more scholarly. The resultant innovations in exegetical principles made the movement a forerunner of later scholarship at several significant points.

Spener and Francke attempted to avoid the appearance of erudition. They wrote in the language of the people, refraining from the use of Latin except in the case of a few scholarly works. In his introduction to the epistle of John, Spener stated his purpose: "My aim in all this work has been only to examine and to interpret most simply what is the intention of the Holy Spirit, and in consequence to indicate clearly the purpose of these instructions for declaring and affirming the faith and to make it fruitful."[17] In preaching he espoused the same, laying aside the usual polemics and subtleties and desiring to communicate and make familiar to his hearers the simple message of the Bible. In order to accomplish this Spener broke from the *Perikopen,* the appointed readings, and began to interpret other parts of the Bible. In this way he was able to give two sermons each time, making it possible to treat entire books of the Bible, including Romans, Corinthians, Ephesians, Colossians, and Galatians.

In addition to the emphasis on expository preaching was a desire to incite the hearer to diligent study of the Holy Scriptures. The Bible was to be read and understood; it became valuable only when used. Rather than advocate a practice such as reading through the entire Bible yearly, which he feared might degenerate into mere mechanics, Spener was more interested in thoughtful reading. He recommended that one begin with prayer, lay hold of what is clear, pass over what cannot be understood, and check with godly ministers and other Christians concerning the meaning of specific passages.[18] In thus warning against the independent reading of the Bible without explanation, Spener attempted to safeguard his emphasis.

Nevertheless, his egalitarianism and freedom of private interpretation undoubtedly led to greater subjectivity, as is connoted by this typical passage from *Spiritual Priesthood:* "When godly hearts come together and read in the Scriptures, each one should modestly and in love tell for the edification of the others what God has enabled him to understand in the Scriptures, and what he thinks will be serviceable for the edification of the others."[19]

Pietism's concern for biblical study was not limited to the common people: biblical theology should become the central discipline among the educated. The Pietists were reacting against a preoccupation which caused dogma to take the place of exegesis. Spener lamented that one could leave the university without having one course in exegesis. Francke maintained that at the time he attended Leipzig one could not even find a copy of the Bible or the New Testament in one of the libraries of the town.[20] There was not a void of commentaries, but the many which were produced aimed primarily to demonstrate how a passage was in agreement with official doctrine. Against this prevailing scholastic mode Spener desired to reinstate biblical studies independent of all systems.

In this desire Pietist scholars evaluated scientific and philological studies positively, and Pietism fostered biblical criticism. Francke differentiated between the shell and kernel of Scripture. Through an emphasis on languages and careful exegesis one must open the shell to get to the kernel. Science, which enables us to do so, is therefore a good and necessary gift of God. But it would be tragic to bite open the shell and throw away the kernel, which comes from inner experience through the Spirit. One must not only come outwardly to an understanding of Scripture, but inwardly to an understanding through the heart, the total being.[21]

Spener and Francke rarely used Greek and Hebrew words in writing because of their desire to communicate and to avoid the appearance of pedantry; yet both were linguistic experts in their own right. Central to their teaching was the conviction that one can best understand the Scriptures by reading them in the original languages. Such ability is not only imperative for the learned but is desirable for all. According to Spener, "it would be a good thing if all Christians would try more earnestly to learn the Hebrew and Greek languages, in which the Scriptures were written and so to understand as far as possible, the Holy Spirit in His own language." Yet such knowledge is not necessary for all. "By the grace of God the Scriptures have been translated into other languages, so that anyone can find enough for the necessary knowledge of Christianity."[22]

In educational circles it was Francke, the pedagogue, who concretized this emphasis through innovative methods. In mastering Greek and Hebrew, one should work with lengthy passages until he is able to translate them. Francke advised that students carry Greek pocket editions with them and look up texts frequently as they are cited. The Hebrew or Greek text should frequently be read aloud. The study of grammar should not be neglected, but should be secondary; for grammatical acquaintance will follow naturally with constant reading and use. He likewise recommended additional reading of the church fathers for advanced students. For example, after progress in Greek and Hebrew the student should commence with biblical Aramaic.[23]

This renewed interest in biblical languages helped undermine the great veneration and slavish adherence to Luther's translation. Spener, who greatly admired Luther's translation, nevertheless defended the right to criticize it; for no translation can ever duplicate exactly the sense of the original. But the cautious Spener disapproved the more open and spectacular criticisms of the straightforward Francke. The latter, against Spener's advice, published monthly his *Observationes biblicae* (1695), our first theological periodical, in which he specifically singled out badly translated passages of Luther and attempted more accurate renditions. The furor which this publication produced was not unexpected.

Two strands evolved from the biblical impulse of Pietism. One neglected serious study as useless and relied exclusively on the Holy Spirit. The other led to the historical approach to the Bible and contributed to the rise of criticism in such followers as Bengel, Anton, Michaelis, and the naturalistically oriented Wolff. The second strand was more consistent with the method of Spener and Francke. Against a traditionalism which permitted little latitude in biblical research, Spener sought free movement in the area of scriptural investigation, exegesis, and application. He pointed to certain passages about which Luther was indecisive. If later Lutheran exegetes had followed Luther's moderation, he felt, fewer doubtful propositions would have been forced on others, and the diligence of all would have been sharpened to investigate more carefully. This emphasis on greater freedom in rational exegesis independent of the authority of the confessions combined with the renewed interest in biblical languages to give new impetus to lower criticism.

At the same time the Pietist view of inspiration, which held that the writers and not the words were inspired by the Holy Spirit, inclined toward higher criticism. The various biblical writers and passages were to be evaluated differently. This led to Spener's struggle with the question of contradictions in the biblical record, to a view on progressive revelation, and to the historical approach to the individual books. In these Pietism often antedated later scholarship. Illustrative of this mood is Francke's outline in his *Guide to the Reading and Study of the Holy Scriptures:*

> Reading, as it respects the LETTER of Scripture, divides itself into three branches: GRAMMATICAL, HISTORICAL, and ANALYTICAL. As it respects the Spirit of the Word, it comprehends four: EXPOSITORY, DOCTRINAL, INFERENTIAL, and PRACTICAL.[24]

The theory of progressive revelation which emerged in Pietism stemmed from the evaluation of biblical materials according to their content and merit. Although Spener attributed all Scripture to divine inspiration and considered both testaments to be the Word of God, he nevertheless differentiated between the two. The New Testament possesses an unequaled brilliance and clarity.[25] In it we have a higher revelation because it fulfills the Old Testament, the Christian experiences it more directly and it raises man to a higher level. Francke substantiated this in his Christological approach to the Bible. Christ is the sum and substance of all Scripture. "The Old Testament has not true relish, if Christ be not understood in it."[26] He is the key to understanding. "Jesus is the very *Soul* of Scripture. . . ."[27]

Even more radical was the insistence of Spener and Francke that the meaning of a passage must be considered in its broader context. At that time the common practice was to isolate words in order to secure from them deductions entirely foreign to their proper meaning. Spener did not so much attribute this to the bad faith of the theologians as to a faulty method. For this reason he insisted that one must "read and examine a text in the entirety of its connection."[28] In a similar way Francke deplored the perplexity which had arisen from the manner in which most people read their Bibles. "They mangle and dismember a text and consider that separately, which should always be connected with antecedents and consequents."[29] In addition to placing passages in context, they must be studied in light of the external circumstances. This approach anticipated later common exegetical assumptions. Not only did it lead to greater study and better understanding, but it also opened the door to the rationalism and individualism which followed.

Supporting the necessity of contextual consideration is Spener and Francke's doctrine of affections. Francke appended "A Treatise on the Affections" to his *Guide to the Reading and Study of the Holy Scriptures*. In it he asserted that an acquaintance with this doctrine is essential to the proper exposition of Scripture. Love, joy, hatred, desire, and other affections are frequently expressed in Scripture by the inspired authors, and we cannot understand them if we are ignorant of these affections. We must "enter into the *feelings* of the Inspired Penmen."[30] In elucidating this position, Francke included long excerpts from Spener's letter to the Philo-Biblical College at Leipzig:

> No practice will prove more pleasant or beneficial, and none more suitable to the College, than after fervent, secret prayer, to discriminate and enter into the Affections of the Inspired Writers with sacred attention and perseverance, and strive to unfold their nature and character. . . . When engaged in the study of the Scriptures, the Idea formed in the Writer's mind should be carefully ascertained; the Affections by which he was influenced; his state of life; and his office at the time he penned the book. . . . Luther again remarks, "that an expositor should, as it were, invest himself with the Author's mind, in order that he may interpret him as another self."[31]

Does not this emphasis on the affections of the writers make light of the work of the Holy Spirit? Francke answered such charges by maintaining that "the Holy Spirit kindled sacred Affections in the Writers' Souls; for it is absurd to suppose, that, in penning the Scriptures, they viewed themselves in the light of mere machines; or that they wrote without *any* feeling or perception. . . ." Here we again discern Pietism's more liberal view which recognized both human and divine elements in the genesis of our Bible. According to Francke, the sacred authors "wrote as they *felt*" at the same time they were "moved by the Holy Ghost."[32]

A common objection raised against this view of affections was that it inevitably would lead to ambiguity in exegesis and hence to complete subjectivism. By referring to various affections one could give to the author what affection he pleased. "This objection is, in truth," Francke reasoned, "a cogent argument in favour of the study of the Affections; for when we have acquired ability to develop them, the Scriptures will, of course, cease to be ambiguous."[33] Similar arguments were to emerge again in debates surrounding biblical criticism; opponents argued that critical study undermines the objective authority of the Bible, while at the same time proponents maintained that such scientific research unveils the heart and truth of the sacred writings.

Practical exegetical implications also rose from the strong primitivism of the early Pietists, namely, their exaltation of the life of the early church. Martin Schmidt believes that this constituted a shift from viewing the Bible as a charter of the Word of God to viewing it simply as a testimony to the historical life of the early community. In thus expanding the canon to encompass the entire apostolic church, there can be a subversion of the authority of the Bible itself.[34] Though one can disagree with Schmidt's conclusion, it is true that such primitivism, with its focus on a holy place in history, was the genesis of a stream of biblical scholarship which has been characterized as *Heilsgeschichte* ("history of salvation"). Johann Bengel (who identified closely with Spener) and his associates first used the word. One can trace two different lines from this advocacy of *Heilsgeschichte*. Because Bengel himself engaged in setting dates in terms of the end of history, one can trace from him a line which extends through Darby and Scofield and in which *Heilsgeschichte* becomes dispensationalism. The other strand comes through Johann Chr. von Hofmann in the nineteenth century and has been revived by Cullmann, Piper, and Dodd in the twentieth. The biblical story is viewed as an expression of God's mighty acts in history, an underlying unity is discerned, and *Heilsgeschichte* is interpreted as the organizing center of all history.

As with other emphases, Pietism's strengths as a corrective movement embodied potential weaknesses. The stress on biblical study for all Christians engendered renewed reverence and interest in the Bible at the same time it led to the perils of private interpretation. Pietism deepened and spiritualized the conception of Scripture in its significance for the Christian life, but this could only be accomplished at the expense of its literal authority. Pietism's doctrine of the internal testimony of the Holy Spirit caused the dead word to become living; but it also opened the door to the mystical excesses of Radical Pietism. Through Bengel and others, Pietism contributed much to later hermeneutics. This same spirit, however, accompanied the rise of German rationalism. From the examination of the views of Spener and Francke it would be unfair to accuse them of many typical individualistic excesses. At the same time, however, it would be inaccurate to deny all such tendencies.

IV

Life or Doctrine: The Centrality of Regeneration and Sanctification

Pietism reiterated the motif that the reformation of doctrine which had been initiated by Luther must be consummated by a new reformation of life. Was this magnification of ethics by Spener and Francke responsible for a new legalistic moralism in the life of the church? Pietism's opponents asserted that it was. They charged Pietism with a new Pelagianism, justification by works, overemphasis on sanctification, and a synergistic view of regeneration. These exaggerated and one-sided emphases, they believed, caused Pietism to degenerate into a moralism which was accompanied by a spirit of legalism, loveless judgment, spiritual pride, and self-sufficiency. Did Pietism exalt its moral preachments above its religious testimony? Was it guilty of the moralistic fallacy of creating a god of goodness instead of responding to the goodness of God? Answers to these basic questions must be sought in an examination of Pietism's attitude toward theology and anthropology and in its soteriological analyses of justification, sanctification, and regeneration.

Theology: Godliness or Dogma?

It has been commonly asserted that Pietism shifted the center of interest from the maintenance of orthodox doctrine to the practice of piety, from the objective form to the subjective appropriation of doctrine precepts, and from the fact of salvation to the moral obligation of the saved. Although Spener was formally orthodox in his theology, his greatest interest was not in orthodoxy of doctrine. Instead, the emphasis of his ministry moved toward practice. *Gottseligkeit* ("godliness"), one of the favorite words of Pietists, triumphed over dogma. There are indeed many statements by Spener and Francke which substantiate this impression. We have seen how the exaltation of the Bible above the Symbolical Books, the differentiation between essentials and nonessentials in dogma, and the preference for biblical instead of systematic theology tended to undermine the authority of the theological formulations of that day.

Moreover, the Pietists often spoke disparagingly of the proud edifice of orthodox dogmatics, which they believed to be pretentious in the claim of finality. Spener deplored the fact that much of the theology of his day remained distant from the people, a wasteland of unintelligible dogma.[1] One of his many innuendos concerning dogmaticians can be found in *Pia Desideria*. "Subtleties unknown to the Scriptures usually have their origin, in the case of those who introduce them, in a desire to exhibit their sagacity and their superiority over others, to have a great reputation, and to derive benefit herein in the world."[2] *Streit* ("quarrelsome") theology, if indeed necessary at all, should be left to university professors alone.[3] In reaction to such polemical theologizing, Spener sometimes appeared to move to the opposite extreme of naive tolerance and dogmatic indifference: "What does it help, if our hearers are free from all papal, Reformed, Socinian, etc. errors, and yet with it have a dead faith through which they are more severely condemned than all those grievously heterodox better lives."[4]

As was true in reference to the Bible, the examination of Pietism's teleological point of view is essential in dealing with the problem of moralism. In his historical novel, Wildenhahn captures Spener's attitude: "All knowledge, all learning, is dead and useless, as long as it does not impart true life to the heart, or promote the cause of practical Christianity."[5] Spener emphasized that which led to edification rather than to accurate definition of traditional dogmas. God cannot be satisfied with incomplete righteousness; he must complete his work. And a person who is truly impelled by the Spirit of God will be able to tell the difference between complete and incomplete righteousness. Such a view led to reflection concerning the effect of individual doctrines on *Seligkeit* ("salvation") and *Gottseligkeit* ("godliness"). Here was an important critical change in which another pragmatic test was introduced. In addition to scriptural criteria, Spener proposed to test each doctrine by whether faith in that doctrine led forth to piety through the grace of God in Christ. Should doctrine be tested by a principle of betterment of life? Is such moral improvement rightly a test of doctrine or a fruit of right faith?

Martin Schmidt maintains that in this teleological shift Spener neglected the paradoxical New Testament teaching that God elects and loves sinners in favor of the more rational proposal that God can acknowledge only a complete righteousness. In this way Spener subjected his own Pauline emphases to rationalistic decay.[6] On the other hand, Schmidt affirms that Spener did uphold a valid New Testament teaching which had not received adequate formulation at the time of the Reformation — the eschatological goal-directedness of Christian existence.[7] Whether Pietism's teleological emphasis was a pragmatism which tested doctrine by humanistic values or whether it was merely a manifestation of the eschatological message of the New Testament is a debatable question. Spener and Francke would have affirmed the latter.

In spite of these practical propensities, the leaders of Pietism professed orthodoxy. They did not desire to disparage doctrine; they insisted that doctrine encompass life. Spener's concern was that the interests of pure doctrine and *Gottseligkeit* be preserved equally and at the same time.[8] As noted, he repeatedly spoke of the pure teaching contained in the Symbolical Books. In spite of his preference for exegesis, he did not intend that Bible study should replace the study of theology. In fact, he frequently used dogmatical studies in order to defend himself in the face of misunderstandings. In Spener's insistence on the agreement of life and doctrine, Max Göbel, one of the best interpreters of Pietism, judges Spener to be as much the enemy of heresy as he was the enemy of ungodliness.[9] Spener, for example, was actually caustic in his attack on Socinianism and atheism.

Consistent with their avowed stance of orthodoxy and true Lutheranism, the Pietist progenitors repudiated any inferences of moralism. Morality separated from a basis of faith, Spener believed, could be treated by the heathen or Turks just as well as or better than by Christians. Mere moral teaching never leads to salvation. "If I preach a hundred years that you should leave the bad and do good," Spener proclaimed, "all is said in vain, where you are not first reborn as a true child of God and from God, for only from this does all goodness flow."[10] In a similar vein, Francke advised that a minister must distinguish "betwixt mere Morality and true Religion; betwixt the moral honest Man and the found Believer, who, from a deep Conviction of the Depravity of his Nature and the Errors of his Life, has learn'd to hate Sin from his Heart, and lives by the Faith of the Son of God."[11]

Martin Schmidt is no doubt accurate in his warning against being misled by Spener's frequent polemic against doctrine in favor of life, for Spener wrote extensively in the field of systematic theology. According to Schmidt, the denial of *Theologiae* was in no way the discarding of all theology, but was the objection to certain features of the method and tradition of "*orthodoxen Streit-Theologiae.*"[12] Instead of charging that Pietism developed no theology because of its emphasis on practice and life, it is more accurate to maintain that it fostered a different theology: namely, a theology of experience, of regeneration, or of devotion. The nature of this theology can be discerned only by the examination of further doctrinal questions.

Man: Savior or Saved?

It has been asserted that the Pietists "tended to gloss

over the depth of sin."[13] In the juridical metaphor of justification which was stressed by Luther, sin and guilt are emphasized and put together in a manner impossible in the biological metaphor of regeneration which was adopted by Spener. In this context some claim that Pietism unconsciously changed from the deep distrust of human nature, which was inherent in classical Protestantism, to an emphasis on concrete individual sins.[14] It was this departure which led them to a much greater optimism concerning the nature of the new life in Christ.

Although this analysis possesses a measure of validity in what is known of the thought of Spener and Francke, it is difficult to substantiate in many of their writings. In fact, the opposite seems to be the case. Spener and Francke held tenaciously to the dogmas of original sin and the human incapacity to do good. In his *"Selbstbiographie"* Spener frequently alluded to his unworthiness, his sinful nature, and his numerous sins.[15] For him the inborn evil was not merely a defect or corruption but was basic sin and guilt. In commenting on the question of the disciples, "Who then can be saved?" (Matthew 19:25), Francke answered, "So great is the Corruption of Man's Nature, so many and great are the Temptations of this World, that indeed it is humanly impossible for any one to be saved."[16] His advice concerning preaching assumed human sinfulness:

> . . . A Minister not only instructs his Hearers what they must do, and how they ought to act, but he also labours fully to apprise and to convince them, by the Evidence of Scripture, of their own native Weakness and Impotency for all that is spiritually good; and that he further shew them, by the same Word of Truth, whom they must look for,

and from whom they may hope to receive all Grace and Strength, not only to renew their Souls in their first Conversion, but also afterwards to enable them to perform every Duty, as well as outward as of inward Religion.[17]

Francke, who often referred to himself as an *elenden Wurm* ("miserable worm"), was more repetitious and insistent than Spener concerning the utter depravity of the soul.

It is true that the Pietist emphasis focused more on the power of sin than on the guilt of sin. It was maintained that the God who is good enough to forgive sin is powerful enough to transform the sinner. Therefore, in addition to the doctrine of original sin, Spener believed that it should be no less emphasized how grace bestows upon the reborn the power to do good. Otherwise, the doctrine of original sin will serve as an excuse for the irresponsibility of some people.[18]

The variations in the anthropology of Spener and Francke did not alter to any significant degree their belief that we are incapable of saving ourselves. We must be saved by God's grace, which is grounded in the merits of Christ. Any righteousness which we have is not sought or inherent, but imputed or forensic. This is the righteousness of Christ which has been reckoned to us and obtained for us through the atonement. But this forensic understanding of the Christ *for* us must be supplemented by the understanding of the Christ working *in* us and *through* us. Such anthropological analysis is necessary for an understanding of Pietism's soteriology.

Soteriology

"The sum of Christianity is repentance, faith, and a new obedience. . . ."[19] Implicit in Spener's definition are the moralistic issues involved in the relationship of law and gospel, faith and works, justification and sanctification, and regeneration.

Law or Gospel?

According to Spener, repentance, which is effected through the Holy Spirit, forms the first stage on the way to salvation. God "calls for the necessity of repentance before faith."[20] Repentance, Spener affirmed in conformity with church doctrine, is penitent knowledge of sin born of knowledge of divine law. Repentance is even more central to Francke's theology. It implies sanctification — the beginning of the laying off of the old man. But knowledge of the law is not enough; no one is converted by the law. Contrition may arise from the law, but no one can attain faith apart from the power of the gospel. In addition to the condemnation of the law, Spener believed that the treasures of salvation offered by God provided the motivation for repentance.

Because of this assertion that law alone cannot effect a right repentance, Spener was attacked as *Gesetzestuerei* ("destroyer of law"). Mediating this accusation is the fact that he was more often called a *Gesetztreiberei* ("legalist") because of his emphasis on works. Although the power for good comes by grace through faith, Spener taught that grace makes use of the law for its purposes. Luther stated that repentance continues throughout life. For Spener this meant that both law and gospel remain effective throughout the lives of believers. Spener advised against anxiety either because of the law or because of neglect of it, because the law is effective not only for controlling the old Adam but also in offering thanks to God. The sayings of Paul against the law are directed to the misuse of the law and not to the law itself. In this way Spener sought to bring law and gospel into organic connection: "It thereby remains that without diminishing the worth of the gospel, the law also has its part in the entire work of God's calling."[21]

This paradoxical relationship between law and gospel produced a doctrine of redemption in which Christ was not only accepted as priest but honored as king.[22] Christianity not only gives forgiveness of sin but also offers to work obedience in us. The view of obedience to Christ as king expands the domain of law to encompass his command, the law of love. In Pietist literature, obedience was commonly defined in terms of *Nachfolge Christi* ("the imitation of Christ"). Francke advised each Christian to "eye continually the Example and Image of Christ, and know assuredly, that he cannot be happier in this World, than when he cometh up to the nearest Conformity with the Image of his Suffering and Crucified Lord."[23]

Nevertheless, Spener sought to differentiate decidedly between *gesetzlich* and *Evangelisch* obedience. The former comes out of the law; the latter comes out of faith and divine love. Legal obedience comes from a person's own power and struggle; evangelical obedience comes from faith and the power of the Spirit.[24] Although Spener attempted in this way to avoid legalism more than Francke, Max Göbel sees in both of these leaders a piety with two sides. One side is genuinely evangelical and against every human compulsion of conscience. The other is legalistic and always in danger of degeneration.[25]

Faith or Works?

Schematically, if not always sequentially, faith follows repentance in Pietism's soteriology. Concerning this keystone of Reformation doctrine, there was frequent affirmation of pure Lutheranism, as can be seen in Spener's *Pia Desideria:*

> We gladly acknowledge that we must be saved only and alone through faith and that our works or godly life contribute neither much nor little to our salvation, for as a fruit of our faith our works are connected with the gratitude which we owe to God, who has already given us who believe the gift of righteousness and salvation. Far be it from us to depart even a finger's breadth from this teaching, for we would rather give up our life and the whole world than yield the smallest part of it.[26]

In substantiating his essential agreement with Spener and Luther that justification by faith alone is the fountainhead from which all other doctrines flow, Francke also added that "every abuse of evangelical doctrine proceeds from its misconception or misapplication."[27]

It was against the alleged misconceptions that the Pietists attempted a reformulation. Against what they believed to be an imaginary and dead faith, Spener and Francke called repeatedly for a living faith, a *seligmachenden Glauben* ("faith which makes blessed").[28] Against a faith which often appeared to be morally indifferent, Spener referred to the Augsburg Confession, which asserted that faith is "not a mere knowledge of histories but a strong powerful work of the Holy Spirit which changes the heart. . . ."[29] Spener and other Pietists often referred to Luther's renowned preface to Romans:

> Faith, however, is a divine work in us. It changes us and makes us to be born anew of God (John 1:13). It kills the old Adam and makes altogether different men of us in heart and spirit and mind and powers, and it brings with it the Holy Spirit. O, it is a living, busy, active, mighty thing, this faith, and so it is impossible for it not to do good works incessantly. It does not ask whether there are good works to do, but before the question rises it has already done them and is always at the doing of them, etc.[30]

In his sermon on the parable of the Pharisee and the publican, Francke defined faith not as a reflection which passes through the mind, but as "a real heavenly and divine light, kindled in our souls by the Holy Spirit, by which we recognize, apprehend, and confide in the grace of our Lord Jesus Christ."[31]

Such definitions of faith are inclusive of good works. Inner works, good motives and virtues, and outward works are but fruit of the sap which the members draw from the vine, Jesus Christ. Good works, for the Pietists, were but marks of true faith. In all such assertions Pietism was conventionally orthodox. But Spener went beyond Orthodoxy when he hinted that such works must necessarily follow. Although he desired to dissociate himself from the formula that good works are necessary for salvation, he practically implied it in the way he spoke of the necessity of an active Christianity. He referred to good works as a *conditio sine qua non,* necessary attributes which inhere in salvation. In a sermon from the year 1697 Spener simply stated that "pure doctrine and holy living must necessarily be united in case of those who want to be saved."[32]

This is indicative of Pietism's desire to bring faith and works into a living relationship. They are not to be confused, but neither are they to be separated. According to Spener, they should not only be considered as cause and effect but also as hidden within one another in a unified and inseparable whole. They are bound together like the sun and its rays. As a fire cannot exist which does not give light and warmth, neither can faith exist which does nothing good.[33]

Martin Schmidt frequently accuses Spener and Francke of synergism, the doctrine that in regeneration the human will cooperates with the Holy Spirit.[34] Though Schmidt would define such an emphasis as both unbiblical and anti-Reformation, there would be others who would define this particular emphasis on the necessity of the response as only, perhaps, anti-Reformation.

Spener felt that Luther had lived in a day which was hungry for grace and which had overrated works. Consequently, the father of the Reformation opposed a trust in the outward nature of *opus operatum* and substituted what is now the classical Protestant formulation of justification by faith. But Spener believed that his own milieu was different. His ministerial colleagues did not have to deal with people who wanted to become blessed from good works as much as with those who regarded them as unnecessary and impossible. Therefore, at one time there must be one emphasis and at another time a different accent. Spener could have had in mind the faith-works issue, as well as the justification-sanctification discussion, when he compared himself with Luther:

> A giant remains great and a dwarf small, and there is no comparison to be made between them; but if the dwarf stands upon the shoulders of the giant, he sees yet further than the giant, since this great stature lifts him above himself. Therefore, it is no wonder that often a dwarf, who is far enough from being a great teacher like Luther, finds something in the Scripture which Luther had not found, after having the advantage of all of Luther's learning, without which he could not have found it.[35]

Justification or Sanctification?

It has been impossible to speak of faith and works, words whose connotations point to the human elements in soteriology, without also treating justification and sanctification, terms which refer more to divine action. As Pietists believed faith and works to be manifest together in living unity, so they spoke of justification and sanctification as bound together in perfect coordination. The forgiveness of sins and the creation of a new person belong together. According to Spener, "not alone justification, but also the creation of a new nature in us and daily renewal belong to the quality of grace and gifts of the gospel."[36]

Nevertheless, Spener did distinguish the two when he spoke of the double office of faith. The first makes us righteous — justification imputed through the work of Christ. The second makes us holy — sanctification mediated through the work of the Holy Spirit. This more technical schematization of double righteousness was not, however, consistently maintained by Pietism's fathers. For the most part, justifying faith was identified rather closely with sanctifying faith.

This coupling together of justification and sanctification created a real problem in the nomenclature of early Pietism. Pietism reiterated the orthodox view that sanctification was a process which followed justification. This is evident in Francke's advice to the preacher:

> Nor is it enough to explain that first and mighty Change, which is at once made in a Sinner at his Conversion, when he comes to love that God which before he hated, and to hate the Evil which he before loved; when from being an Unbeliever he becomes a Believer; or when his false and dead Faith is changed into a true and saving one: But that further progressive Change should also be much recommended, in which the Christian must be improving to the very End of his Life.[37]

If sanctification is a process which follows conversion, and if sanctification and justification are bound together, what does this do to the once-for-all nature of the act of justification? Spener was consistent in following through the logic of this position. To him, justification "must always be continued, as if it were a steadily continuing act."[38] We must allow the justifying and canceling of sins and the sanctifying power of Christ to continue to work in us at the same time. In this Spener deviated from the orthodox conception of justification as *declaratio iustificatio* ("declared justification"). According to Grünberg, Spener had in mind the condition of justification; his opponents, the ideal act of justification. His orthodox counterparts saw in it a conclusive moment in itself. Spener viewed it as a continuing side of the Christian appropriation of salvation. Spener viewed it as a continuing side of the Christian appropriation of salvation. Grünberg thus concluded that in reference to the momentary act Spener often confused sanctification and regeneration. He joined together justification and sanctification when he should have joined justification and regeneration.[39] Francke, who placed a much greater emphasis on the conversion experience, was not as prone to do the same.

Whatever change was effected in Pietism's doctrine of justification came as a result of its great emphasis on sanctification. Because sanctification carried fewer moralistic connotations than works, Spener was even more bold in proclaiming its necessity. "As the faith, which alone justifies us and makes holy, is inseparable from good works, so no one will be justified other than those who are intent upon sanctification."[40]

It was in the context of this doctrine that Spener's orthodox opponents charged him with the heresy of *Vollkommenheit* ("perfectionism"). It is true that Spener used the term. In his small treatise on perfection, *Von dem Tempel Salomons*, he argued that perfection is a valid biblical and traditional doctrine.[41] He wished to free it, however, from two traditional abuses. One taught the impossibility of perfection, and the other sought to find it in the wrong places.[42] As he held to the hope of better times for the church because of his belief that God fulfills his promises, so he expected a measure of perfection for the regenerate. In *Pia Desideria*, Spener asserts the desirability of achieving perfection; at the same time he concedes that

. . . here in this life we shall not manage that, for the farther a godly Christian advances, the more he will see that he lacks, and so he will never be farther removed from the illusion of perfection than when he tries hardest to reach it. . . . Meanwhile, even if we shall never in this life achieve such a degree of perfection that nothing could or should be added, we are nevertheless under the obligation to achieve some degree of perfection.[43]

This intriguing insight, that those who seek perfection are removed from the illusion of it, is similar to Wesley's testimony which claimed the experience of perfection for others but not for himself. Franz Hildebrandt observes that Spener likewise anticipated Wesley's doctrine of perfection in the distinction between "having" sin and "doing" sin.[44] Only those who commit sin consciously are those who "do" sin.[45]

Francke followed Spener in pointing out the paradoxical nature of the doctrine of perfection. He repeatedly spoke of his own sin and warned against the illusion of one's own perfection. At the same time he was certain that to some degree perfection can be attained by the Holy Spirit working in us and through us. In *Von der Christen Vollkommenheit* ("Concerning Christian Perfection") he posited the paradox:

Therefore it follows that to a certain extent that both are true; we are perfect, and we are not perfect. Namely, we are perfect through Christ and in Christ through justification and imputation of the righteousness of Jesus Christ. However, we are not and never will be entirely perfect. . . .[46]

Such passages illustrate the fallacy of some of the extreme charges against Pietism while at the same time revealing evidence which can partially validate the frequent accusations of perfectionism.

Regeneration

When Spener wanted to speak precisely, he distinguished

the momentary creation of a new person, regeneration, from the progressive working out of the principle of life thereby established, sanctification. Regeneration held a central place in his soteriology. As we have seen, Martin Schmidt and others designate it the *locus classicus* (classical source) of Pietist theology. Regeneration was for Spener what justification had been for Luther, and he began his ministry at Berlin with sixty-two sermons on *Wiedergeburt*. The "born again" figure of speech, which has remained popular in many strands of Protestantism, has strong roots in German Pietism. For Spener this biological Johannine and Pauline metaphor represented a completion and enhancing of the equally biblical juridical metaphor of justification.

In the mysterious process of regeneration there is a moment of complete passivity in a person which gives room to the omnipotent working of God. The decisive metaphor which serves as an approximation of Luther's *sola gratia* ("grace alone") is not birth, but conception.[47] In a similar repudiation of the synergistic risk inherent in his theology, Spener distinguished the diligence which is human from the power which is divine. Regeneration results in the overcoming and eradication of sin and the participation in the divine nature, which is the formation of oneself in the likeness of Jesus. Through this birth Jesus Christ acquires form in each believer. Christ has thus effected a victory over Satan.[48]

Inherent to this revivified emphasis on regeneration was the temptation to stereotype the regenerate and the unregenerate. Although Spener usually emphasized the fluidity of the boundaries which exist between the renewed and unrenewed, he did often use more exact distinctions, as in his division of theologians into regenerate and unregenerate.[49] Francke, however, made an even sharper distinction between the converted and the unconverted. Abetting this tendency was Pietism's assumption that regeneration is necessary for all but those who remain steadfast in baptismal grace, and Spener even inferred that nearly everyone falls from that grace sometime during life. In a similar way, these distinctions were encouraged by the insistence that an unregenerate person is incapable of ever completely discerning spiritual truths. Grünberg mentions the insufficiency of traditional labels in the controversies surrounding this issue. Each side accused the other of Pelagianism. Spener so accused his opponents because they held the natural unregenerate person to be capable of grasping divine mysteries. His opponents charged him with Pelagianism because he admitted a certain knowledge of the Bible to be possible apart from the illumination of the Holy Spirit.[50] Many of these discussions which claimed that regeneration is necessary for proper understanding of spiritual truth anticipated the epistemological "leap of faith" of later existentialism. In the context of his doctrine of affections, Francke stated it another way: ". . . the mind of Christ best explains the mind of Christ."[51]

In perspective, one beholds consistently in the writings and thought of these early Pietist leaders the effort to avoid the appearances and errors of moralism. Yet one sees in the teleological test of doctrine a moralistic temptation. Pietism's anthropology contained liberalizing tendencies in its pluralization and consequent minimization of sin. The shift from the judging function of the law and the commandments to their role as requirements of Christian life tended toward legalism. The application of the sanctification test to the justification experience led in many cases to greater subjectivization. And the attempted classification of people into regenerate and unregenerate contained the potential seeds of prideful self-assertion. In spite of such pitfalls, the ethical thrust of Pietism was not cast in the medieval Catholic framework of the meritorious works required for salvation as much as in the biblical framework of faith, justification, holiness, righteousness, sanctification, and regeneration.

V

Human Spirit or Holy Spirit: The Theology of Experience

*Pietism has often been designated as a theology of experi-*ence. Scholars have differed and vacillated in determining which is the primary motif of Pietism — regeneration or the focus on the charismatic doctrine of the Holy Spirit. We have already noted the preference for empirical knowledge in Spener's exaltation of the dogma of experience. Francke would desire each of us to "have a true Sense of the gracious Operations of the Holy Spirit in our Souls, and know experimentally, that God of a Truth has erected his Kingdom in our Souls, which consists in Righteousness, Peace and Joy in the Holy Ghost."[1] The language of such theology has included such terms as illumination, the inner man, emotionalism, and *Busskampf* (penitential struggle). In his comparative study of Pietism and Methodism, Professor Nagler viewed such religious empiricism as the most important contribution of both movements.[2] Others have credited (or blamed) Pietism as a progenitor of both Schleiermacherian liberalism and revivalistic fundamentalism because of their common epistemological focus on experience.

Pietism has frequently been labeled as mystical. The problem with such a characterization is that there is even greater confusion regarding the word "mysticism" than there is for "Pietism." The early Pietists recognized this. Joachim Lange, one of their chief apologists, warned that all brands of mysticism should not be regarded with equal worth, "for one finds in many [brands] more wood, hay, and stubble than gold, silver, and precious stones."[3] Though "mysticism" may be defined simply as "the experience of direct contact with God," the variations in its usage and connotations are legion. A speculative type of mysticism is found in Neoplatonic and theosophic theories about a ladder of ascent to God and in the idea that individuals are microcosms, each participating in a little world which reproduces the great world, or macrocosm. In contradistinction to the speculative types of mysticism are the practical or affective types in which there is not so much a union of metaphysical substance as a union of wills and affections, like that of Francis of Assisi and his devotional identification with the way of Christ. In ascetic mysticism, one achieves union of soul with God through purgation of the fleshly and the material; in worldly mysticism, one finds union with God through union with His creation and service to His creatures. There are "acting" types of mysticism in which the individual takes the primary initiative, and there are "reacting" types like the quietist abandonment of self in which the individual allows God to operate. Some mystics refer to a union in which the human soul is absorbed in the Godhead; others think in relational language and speak of communion or conversation in which the discontinuity between the person and God is maintained. A distinction can also be made between autonomous mysticism and mysticism in which the mystical experience is checked by other criteria. In German theology the first has often been named *Mystik*, a phenomenon not necessarily Christian, and the second, *Mystische Theologie*, is a mysticism joined more with tradition and churchly life. It may seem obvious that Pietists have been identified more with the practical, reacting, communion, and *Mystische Theologie* types; nevertheless, it is in this context that we must deal with some of the primary problems of Pietism.

It is evident that the empirical and mystical strands in Pietism are germane to the problem of subjectivism — the exaltation of the human spirit above the Holy Spirit. For Pietism, was experience the source of revelation or primarily a product of revelation? Are feelings, joys, and conversion experiences the means to faith, or are they the fruit of faith? The Pietists reacted against a theology based upon correct understanding of concepts. Did they move too far in the opposite direction by replacing empiricism of mind with empiricism of feeling? Pietism packaged its mystical streak through its stress on the illumination of the Holy Spirit. Did this mean a revival of so-called mystical errors, in which individual revelations came to be exalted above the special revelation of Christ? Did such introspection reduce the Holy Spirit to a mere projection of the human spirit? The early Pietists alluded frequently to the inner man. Did they thus develop anthropological centers which undermined the theocentric orientation of theology? And did not the rediscovery of the individual's relationship to God so personalize religion that it became overly emotionalized? Is it correct to charge Pietism with an exaggeration of feelings which results in a cheapening familiarization with God? Pietism sought assurance and joy. De we have in this an early manifestation of success-oriented "peace of mind" movements? Pietism preached for conversion. Did the experiential accoutrements of conversion — the penitential struggle and the dated experience — prescribe the way of salvation in such a way as to result in self-righteousness and legalism? Such questions must be considered in any evaluation of the charismatic side of Pietism.

Illumination

Of Spener's favorite words, the various forms of *Erleuchtung* ("illumination" or "enlightenment") are among the most used. In the theology of Pietism this illumination transforms dead faith into living faith. Spener emphasized the illumination of the Holy Spirit in contradistinction to human wisdom. The living faith is from the light of the Holy Spirit; "the dead faith comes from human power and reason."[4] Consistent with Pietism's repudiation of rationalism was Spener's wish that all reason "be taken captive among those obedient to Christ."[5] He did allow that some knowledge of doctrine and Scripture is possible apart from repentance, regeneration, sanctification, and the illumination of the Spirit, but the great stress on the latter together with the depreciation of reason tended to exalt revelational theology above natural theology. In this, Pietists felt they shared Luther's epistemological repudiation of Aristotelianism and the philosophical quest for God.

In spite of this rejection of philosophy, the doctrine of illumination constituted an opening wedge for a resuscitation of natural theology. It was possible for illumination to become a medium to God apart from Christ, the creeds, or the church. This was especially the case in Spener's view of visions, dreams, raptures, angelology, miracles, and special revelations. Commenting upon the celebrated case of a young lady of nobility who had claimed special revelations, Spener summarized his views. He believed both Testaments affirm that God has revealed himself through dreams, voices, and visions. In opposition to scholars who taught that revelation ended with the apostles in the New Testament, Spener asserted that the prophetic light of God continues to shine, although not in the same measure. Just as false and true prophets needed to be differentiated in the Old Testament, each new case also needs to be examined. Each revelation is either human fraud, the deception of the Devil, the fantasy of man, or the revelation of God. He minimized the first two options but remained open concerning the two remaining alternatives. The best test is found in Acts 5:8: "If the work be of man, it will fail; but if it is from God, nothing can defeat it."[6] The primary criterion for special revelation is that it must not be contrary to Scripture. Though he was certain that the miracles of Christianity are not limited to the past but continue to occur, as in the miracle of the regeneration of the old into the new creature, Spener remained noncommittal concerning his ability to distinguish the natural from the supernatural in many of the psychological and physiological manifestations of human spiritual life.

It was in his belief that there dwells in every person *das göttliche Licht* ("the godly light" which gives us the power to distinguish the ways of God from the ways of the flesh) that Spener gave the greatest impetus to natural theology. In his Master's dissertation he defined rather broadly the ability of the natural light to discover God. Though he accepted natural theology throughout his life, in no way was it the determinative element in his epistemology. He analogized that the natural knowledge of God is to the light of revelation as the light of a piece of damp firewood is to the rays of the sun. Natural knowledge of God must always be subordinated to knowledge from revelation. We can know some things through our reason, dreams, and special experiences, but true saving knowledge cannot be obtained in this way.[7] It is only in Christ that we know God.

The knowledge gained through illumination was for the early Pietists less important than the fundamental purpose of God's enlightenment — to become united in fellowship with God and brothers and sisters rather than with the being of God. From my perspective, Donald Bloesch is right in his assertion that for evangelical Pietism communion and fellowship are more significant than the concept of identity.[8] Though they kept personal diaries and attempted to revitalize their personal devotional lives, the Pietists' greater affirmation was on fellowship rather than solitude in the life of the Christian. The holiness and sovereignty of God were stressed more than the beatific vision. Illumination involves prayer and adoration, but it is the illuminating spirit which makes a difference in the life of the Christian.

The Inner Person

We have examined the doctrine of the inner testimony

of the Holy Spirit as it relates to scriptural authority. Next we need to look at the charismatic implications. Pietist literature is replete with phrases such as "the indwelling Christ," "the inner meaning" of doctrines and sacraments, "the inner man," and "inward or personal Christianity." In *Pia Desideria* Spener synthesized the ethical and the mystical in his hyperbole that "our whole Christian religion consists of the inner man or new man." He expanded this in a rather lengthy passage:

> One should therefore emphasize that the divine means of Word and sacrament are concerned with the inner man. Hence it is not enough that we hear the Word with our outward ear, but we must let it penetrate to our heart, so that we may hear the Holy Spirit speak there, that is, with vibrant emotion and comfort feel the sealing of the Spirit and the power of the Word. Nor is it enough to be baptized, but the inner man, where we have put on Christ in Baptism, must also keep Christ on and bear witness to him in our outward life. Nor is it enough to have received the Lord's Supper externally, but the inner man must truly be fed with that blessed food. Nor is it enough to pray outwardly with our mouth, but true prayer, and the best prayer, occurs in the inner man. . . .[9]

Add to this emphasis on the inner person Spener's favorite polemic against *opus operatum* ("automatic efficacy") of outward observances, and it becomes evident that his language bears the marks of spiritualistic and mystical theologies. How much he read his own conservative theological orientation into the nomenclature of mysticism remains the basic question of his anthropology.

An inward look involves the search for or an assumption of an anthropological center. Pietism located this in the heart. In many of his sermons, Spener laid down the principle that religion is an affair of the heart. Concerning the service of Christ he wrote, "I do want it to be not a mere empty thought but one dwelling truly in the heart."[10] Francke's frequently quoted testimony of his own condition as a student is indicative of the same. "I kept my theology in my head and not in my heart, and it was much more a dead science than a living knowledge. I knew to be certain how to say well what is faith, regeneration, justification, renewal, etc., but of them all there existed nothing in my heart."[11] In prayer he pleaded for a sincerity devoid of elegant phrases because "God regards the Sense of the Heart, rather than the Language of the Lips."[12] Francke often regarded the heart as the place of God's dwelling.

It is difficult to discern the meaning and various shades of connotation which the word "heart" carried in Pietist usage. Though their usage contained definite overtones of emotionalism, antirationalism, and individualism, these early Biblicists employed the term primarily because of its scriptural rootage, and for this reason the term may have pointed more to singleness of purpose, purity of motive, and wholeness of personality. In popular discourse Spener and Francke often substituted the term "soul" for "heart," and in more learned endeavors they employed the word "will" as a scholarly synonym. In contradistinction to the orthodox, who viewed the intellect as the human organ in which God's grace first begins to work, Pietism regarded the conversion of the will as primary.

In these designations, Pietism was guilty of abetting the idea of unusual anthropological centers — the idea which became so prevalent in later examinations of the psychology of religion. Grünberg, however, claims there is evidence "that Spener was striving to place intellect and will in an inner relationship and recognized their reciprocal dependence better than his opponents and traditional dogmatics."[13] Spener did perceive that divine enlightenment affects our understanding as well as our will, and he often spoke of regeneration as remaking not only the will but also the entire person.[14] A more organismic view might also be deduced from Spener's dynamic view of faith in which faith as *fiducia* ("trust"), as *notitia* ("conception"), and as *assensus* ("assent") must be joined. Although we will see in what is to follow that Francke's theology depends more on the exaltation of the heart as the special seat of the emotions, Spener's writings reveal that for him the term represented an attempt to sense the working of God through the total person.

Does such internalization represent an individualization of the working of the Holy Spirit? We have already noted in considering the doctrine of the church that Martin Schmidt declares that Spener's usage of the word *Erbauung* ("edification") deviated from the Pauline metaphor of building up the whole body. Instead, he claims, Spener emphasized the "edification of the inner man."[15] Francke especially seemed to move in this direction. While such a charge finds enough validation in the writings of Spener and Francke to show a subjective shift, one must consider this shift in the context of Pietism's total doctrine of the church. Pietism focused on the person primarily because it regarded individual regeneration as the means for the reformation of the entire church. It is interesting to observe that in the rather lengthy passage quoted above from *Pia Desideria,* Spener repeatedly used "*unser* [our] *inner-*

liche Mensch." Spener was far too orthodox in his doctrine of the church to be guilty of extreme individualism.

Schmidt likewise maintains that in the doctrine of the inner man Pietism followed the spiritualists whose stress began with the primacy of inner things and proceeded to encompass the effect on the outward and the bodily. Luther, however, began with the outer Word, which in turn has its consequence for the inner life. For Luther, the new person is created in justification; for Pietism, in regeneration. For this reason, Schmidt believes, Spener failed to make clear the absolute necessity of the sacraments and the Word for the new creation.[16] The validity of this critique can be seen in Spener's claim that the inner man does influence the outer man; its falsity is seen in Spener's teaching that the inner man is in the first place produced from without, that is, from God. "The inner man which God produced in regeneration has come to be the outer man."[17] Overall, Schmidt is no doubt accurate in his implication that the movement from the inner to the outer, even when effected by the Spirit, leads in different directions than Luther's stress on continual dependence on the outer Word.

Spener also made the distinction between *fides quae creditur* ("faith in which we believe"), and *fides qua creditur* ("faith by which we believe"). Some claim that in this distinction he turned his attention from the object of faith to the believing person. But Spener desired both true knowledge and true faith. True believers are those who are not only correct in reference to the articles of faith but also in relation to the inner nature of their faith.[18] In this aspect of its anthropology, Pietism was responsible for a new focus being placed on the inner person. It claimed, however, that such exaltation of the human spirit was but the proper work of the Holy Spirit.

Emotionalism

Koppel Pinson gives a dramatic digest of a patriotic sermon delivered by Schleiermacher in 1813:

> His entire sermon was one torrent and each word emanated from the times and was for the times. When, after addressing the young recruits with all the fire of his enthusiasm, he turned to the mothers and concluded with the words, "Blessed be your bodies which bore such sons, blessed be your breasts that gave such children to suck," the whole assemblage was seized with convulsions and amidst loud weeping and sobbing Schleiermacher pronounced his final Amen.[19]

Although such phenomena would not have been as probable in the context of the preaching of Spener and Francke, early Pietism was soon regarded as a catalyst of emotions. Heinrich Westphal was not atypical in what he wrote to his former teacher, Francke: "But I know God to be another. His true heart I know and have experienced. I embrace him with the most passionate love."[20] Pietists emanating from Halle soon came to examine their emotions and the hearts of others in diaries, letters, and personal interviews, and it has been surmised that the later sentimentality of the eighteenth century was a secular manifestation of Pietist *Frömmigkeit* ("piety"). Even with Spener and Francke there are indications that the internalization of the doctrine of illumination led to an intensification of feelings which penetrated Pietism's theology of experience.

Although the prosaic and calm Spener was not given to emotional excitation, he did write of the *Empfindung* ("feeling" or "sensation") of faith. He believed feelings to be the experience of grace, and he taught that a certain measure of feeling should be associated with faith. Spener also taught that some feel this inner comfort of salvation to a higher degree than others. In the exegetical principle that a proper development of affections is necessary for correct understanding of the Bible, Spener and Francke, who developed this view in more detail, opened the door to an introspective nurture and classification of feelings. In spite of these Spenerian motifs, it is Francke who is held most responsible for the emotionalism in Pietism. To the question "What is the love of God?" Francke responded, "It is of such a nature, that it must be felt, in order to be understood."[21] He frequently spoke of "cheerful faith," "warmed hearts," and "great joy" because "Religion is by no means a grievous and melancholy thing, but full of Pleasure and greatly desirable even for its own Sake."[22]

This accentuation of the joyful fruits of faith added to Francke's thought a pragmatic thrust in which happiness and success were promised as the result of an active faith. In the account of his prodigious labors in *Pietas Hallensis*, Francke regarded faith as a living principle which enabled him to undertake with a full assurance of success any enterprise which promised to do good. When the going was the roughest, he believed ". . . the Lord would undoubtedly give us another Instance of his Providence."[23] In answer to those who were critical of this asking for material things he replied, "Did not the Apostle Paul ascribe the contributions made for the saints, at his suggestion, to the hand of the Lord?"[24] In a later sermon Francke developed this pragmatic approach:

> I say, where Faith is thus known in the Light of God's Spirit, and a Man experiences it to be so in his Heart, then he sees at the same time that the Fruit and Advantage of that Faith . . . is of so large a compass, as to contain all the good things we can conceive or hope for from God. . . .[25]

Historian Isaac Dorner, who criticized Lutheran orthodoxy for its tendency to dwell on the principle of pardon, was equally severe on Pietism, in which a more active faith was unable to break through the limitations of the ego.[26]

It would be false, however, to identify Pietism completely with emotionalism or a theology of success. Although Spener knew how to speak the language of his mystically oriented friends, he read into this language his own ethical interests. Spener was too reasonably and practically constituted to place the chief value on immediate experience. Although he wrote about feeling, he confessed that he himself had not experienced any prominent sensations and that "true belief is not so much felt emotionally as known by its fruits of love and obedience to God."[27] Feelings are often changeable and unreliable; lack of spiritual peace does not mean a person has fallen from grace. In fact, Spener observed that many righteous Christians complain that the inability to experience faith emotionally is one of their most burdensome sorrows.

Even many of Francke's statements rejected extreme emotionalism, as can be seen in an extract from his memoirs:

> You may possibly suppose, that love to God consists in a

good emotion or desire, which you may sometimes feel, especially when you pray, and that after this you may sin again. But this, dear children, is not love. Love is constant and unchanging, and is to be discovered by your obedience to God, and your patience under trials, rather than by your feelings.[28]

Likewise, Francke protested against the tendency to intensify feelings by self-imposed means. He tempered his theology of success with his equally strong emphasis on the demands of obedience and even went so far as to suggest that obedience to the demands of righteousness ought to displace dependence upon "sweet emotions" which can be felt only at certain times.[29]

It would be fallacious to attempt to deny the seeds of emotionalism in Spener's thought or Francke's charismatic personality, but it is possible to confirm Max Weber's analysis that ". . . it is very one-sided to make this emotional element the distinguishing characteristic of Pietism as opposed to Lutheranism."[30] Likewise, a broader perspective will not only point to negatively regarded emotional excesses but also to Pietism's recognized contributions to hymnody and devotional literature. Another factor necessary for a conclusive evaluation of the extent of emotionalism in Pietism is the recognition of the basic cleavage between Pietism's two founding leaders. On this matter, more than any other, it is important to recognize the differences between the even-tempered Spener and the exuberant Francke. The personality of the latter was either the cause or the result of an experiential theology. This was especially true of Francke's doctrine of conversion and *Busskampf*.

Busskampf ("Penitential Struggle") and Conversion

Francke's theology of conversion accompanied his own *grosse Wende* ("great change") which occurred at Lüneberg in 1687. The following excerpts from his own account reveal the struggle which was to become a prototype in later Pietist soteriology:

> I now realized earnestly that I found not in myself such faith as I would set forth in the sermon. This weighed on me heavily. . . . The more I wanted to help myself with reason the deeper I plunged into unrest and doubt. . . . This misery caused many tears to come to the eyes. . . . In *solcher grosser Angst* [great anxiety] I threw myself on my knees and cried once again to God. Then God heard me. So great was his love that he did not want to take away gradually my doubt and unrest, of which I would have been pleased, but he heard me suddenly. As one turns over his hand, so was all my doubt taken away. I was certain in my heart of the grace of God in Christ Jesus. I could not only name God, God, but also my Father. I stood up with an entirely different disposition. I bended to my knees with worry and doubt; I arose with unexpressible joy and great wisdom. I was so filled with joy that I couldn't sleep. It was as if I had lived all of my life in a dream and now awoke for the first time. I felt that I had been dead but had become alive. I could not remain in bed but sprang to praise God. My reason stood as it were afar. For the streams of living water had come to me so much that I could easily forget the stinking mist pools of the world.[31]

This experience and testimony became the seed for the language of revivalistic Pietism, which came to include such terms as *Empfindlichkeit* ("sensitiveness") of standing grace, *Gnadendurchbruch* ("piercing through of grace"), conviction of sin, dated conversion, and *Busskampf*. Francke has often been accused of viewing his own sudden conversion as the norm for all conversions. According to Francke, everyone should move through a similar penitential struggle in preparation for conversion, and he advised preachers to ask others ". . . if they have had a lively and affecting Sense of the Corruption of their own Hearts, and of the Misery of the natural State?"[32]

To the extent that this is representative of his real opinions, Francke is at variance with Spener, whose religious life developed without sudden transitions, struggles, storms, or stresses. Spener believed the ways of God are different with each individual. With one person conversion is gradual; with another it is sudden. For this reason he did not feel that penitential pains were prerequisite to conversion. Although he frequently used terms such as "broken-heartedness" and "break-through," he was hesitant to support any schematization of the works of repentance. Continually emphasizing individual difference, he concentrated more on noticing evidence of moral transformation, which a true conversion must show, than on controlling or intensifying the experience of repentance.[33]

Francke's biographers take issue with any sharp antitheses proposed between Pietism's two foremost leaders. Erich Beyreuther maintains that there is nothing unhealthy, nothing "enthusiastic" in Francke's conversion. "If there is, then the Biblical message about conversion should be designated as unhealthy and enthusiastic."[34] Beyreuther continues this apology by referring to Francke's reply in his later life to the inquiry of a student. The student wondered whether it was necessary to know a certain time as the moment of conversion. Francke's answer destroys some common caricatures.

We do not ask, "Are you converted? When were you converted?" But we ask, "What does Christ mean to you? What have you experienced personally with God? Is Christ necessary to you in your daily life?" And it is, to be certain, very likely that one does not know at all the period of time. . . .[35]

Erhard Peschke proposes that Francke allowed that we may not know the exact day, week, or month of our conversion, but we should at least know the year.[36] Whatever later adjustments Francke made in this regard, it is nevertheless true that his dramatic conversion experience and his introspective analyses of feelings of guilt, anxiety, sorrow, and joy resulted in a greater emotionalization and subjectivism in his theology of experience than in the theology of Spener.

Pietism's theology of experience was vulnerable to some of the charges of subjectivism. Its doctrine of illumination sometimes separated the Holy Spirit from the Word in such a way as to eliminate some sharp distinctions between human spirit and Holy Spirit. Its view of the inner person aided the rise of the anthropocentricity which Barth has opposed in our century. And Pietism's emphasis on feelings easily became an emotionalism which led to an excessive preoccupation with self as well as an artificial excitation of feelings as a way to God. In general, however, defenders of Pietism argue that in it we have a genuine revival of the doctrine of the Holy Spirit. Pietism's theology makes experience more a receptive medium than a productive source of revelation. It is asserted that the corrective influence of Pietism was necessary to point to the truth we are experiencing today — the truth that feelings are a valid part of life, that the response of the total person is to be affirmed, and that the charismatic nature of the church can be neglected only at the peril of losing something valuable from our Christian unity. The context of the thought of early Pietism reveals that for them experience was much more the appropriation of than the substitution for revelation.

VI

World Negating or World Affirming: The Attitude Toward the Secular

How did the early Pietists resolve the recurring paradoxical motif in discipleship; that is, to be in but not of the world? In Johannine thought, the world is identified by its fallenness and opposition; yet this same world is the object of God's love and redemption. The church is the people of God called out from the world through Christ; but at the same time it is the priestly and prophetic people sent forth into the world by Christ. On the one hand, the church has to purge itself from secularization and worldliness; on the other hand, it has to become worldly to witness and to be of service to the real needs and concerns of the world.

Pietism has commonly been regarded as having shifted its weight to the world-negating side of this polarity. It has been accused of gathering in pious conventicles rather than praising God in the midst of the world; of fleeing rather than conquering the sinful world; and of retreating to the world of private piety rather than facing social responsibility. Pietism's ethic has been said to be limited to individual configurations; even its social effects, it has been maintained, have not been intentionally attained as much as they have incidentally evolved as by-products of its inner life. Such characterizations find a degree of validation in Spener's asceticism and Francke's espousal of self-denial. But this is not the total picture. Pietist eschatology and philanthropic activity introduce another dimension. A fair evaluation can be constructed only from a comprehensive anaylsis of Pietism's motif concerning the denial of the world, its doctrine concerning the end of the world, and its sense of mission in the world.

Denial of the Pleasures of the World

Many caricatures of Pietists resemble the one given in Wildenhahn's sympathetic nineteenth-century novel about Spener, in which this description comes from the mouth of an opponent: "A Pietist is one who regards it as a mortal sin to wear an embroidered handkerchief and a wig; one who fasts every other day and wears shabby garments; one who talks from morning till night about godliness, and who, on Wednesdays and Saturdays, attends Spener's conventicle."[1] It is fair to conjecture that such ascetic Pietist tendencies originated in Spener himself. When he was twelve he was induced to join in a dance. His serious nature together with his godmother's strong admonitions against frivolities caused him to be overtaken by pangs of conscience, and, as he later reported, he broke away, never to dance again. Preoccupied in study, Spener's university days were devoid of the usual dancing, fencing, drinking, and fighting. From this many deduce that it was natural that his later teachings contained admonitions against the theater, playing cards, jewelry, and *Putzes* ("finery of apparel"). Spener designated as one of the marks of a Pietist the willingness "to give up freedom in questionable little things. . . ."[2] He espoused moderation in dress, food, and drink.

Of interest is Spener's fairly lengthy statement on drinking in the *Pia Desideria*.[3] Pointing to the prevalence of drunkenness in high and low places, he lamented that this state was never recognized as something which requires repentance. There were a few who did regard drunkenness as a sin, but the fact that there were so few, he felt, made it all the more dangerous. Appropriating the apostle Paul's admonition against drunkenness, and arguing from the analogy of adultery, Spener maintained that it is wrong to get tipsy or drunk even once for the sake of a toast to a friend's health. Theodore Tappert, who translated *Pia Desideria* into English, mistakenly translated *einem Rausch zu trinken Gelegenheit* as "to drink occasionally" rather than "to get tipsy or drunk occasionally."[4] Consequently, the impression is given that Spener was moving in the direction of total abstinence. Regardless of our present convictions, it is important to report accurately that it was drunkenness (whether occasionally or even just once) and not occasional drinking which Spener opposed. The emergence of a brewery as one of the enterprises at Halle indicates that early Pietism was less extreme than the later temperance movement.

In spite of the brewery, however, it was the Halle milieu of Francke and his followers that bequeathed to Pietism its ascetic reputation. Illustrative of this atmosphere are the regulations from Francke's *Scriptural Rules for Living*:

> Do not speak much.
> Trifling jests and anecdotes, do not become a Christian.
> When you are in conversation, avoid speaking of yourself, or desiring to do so.
> Avoid unnecessary mirth. All laughter is not sinful, but it should be a mark of a peaceful, and joyful, and not a trifling state of mind. If others laugh at foolish jests, and improper expressions, do not join with them.
> Engage in no unprofitable work; for you shall give account of every moment of your time, and of the manner in which it has been employed.
> Read no trifling nor useless books, for the sake of passing away time.[5]

However, it should be pointed out that Francke's students were permitted much greater freedom in the expression of their childish energy than was customary for his day. His institutions rejected the commonplace beatings with sticks and severe punishments which in other schools accompanied the teachers' cathartic fits of anger. Though the rules were strict, infractions were not as severely penalized because the schools focused more on practical education and moral supervision in an atmosphere of love. Francke's colleague Joachim Lange, speaking of the dance, opera, and comedy, did move further in the ascetic direction: "I have proved crystal clear that such things are through and through nothing other than vanity of vanities, an unreasonable and unchristian nature, even if they remain free of gross excesses."[6] It is easy to understand how Halle Pietism under Francke's son degenerated into a sterile legalism once the initial evangelical enthusiasm and zeal had waned.

Such prohibitions are symptomatic of Pietism's devaluation of culture in general. Francke devalued "the Arts and Learning of this World."[7] Many have judged Spener to be partly responsible for the negative attitude of later Pietism to aesthetics and art, but such a view needs to be balanced by the recognition of Spener's more worldly interest in heraldry. Any Pietist suspicions of worldly culture, however, did not apply to worldly work. The Pietist, like the Calvinist, fostered an *innerweltliche Askese* ("inner worldly asceticism"). Intense piety came to be associated with self-disciplined industriousness. Max Weber cited Pietism as an illustration of his basic thesis concerning the influence of Protestantism on capitalism by noting the preference of employers for those from Pietist backgrounds.[8] While it is easy to overstate Weber's thesis, it is true that Pietism fostered an ethical stance which sanctified activities in all of life. That the Pietists were suspicious of particular activities in entertainment and culture probably stemmed from their insistence that all be done for God's glory and the neighbor's good.

Fundamental to this discussion is the question of whether some of the moralistic regulations stemmed from a type of Neoplatonic dualism. Did Pietism regard the desires of the body as peculiarly evil? Some have suspected such Greek tendencies in the frequent warnings against the lusts of the flesh. We have seen that Spener and Francke appropriated the classifications of inner and outer, higher and lower, and spiritual and fleshly in such a way as to be suspect of a departure from the Hebraic holistic view of persons. Yet there are many indications that these Pietist leaders fit such terms into Pauline categories, which replace the Greek body-soul dualism with the dualism between a person *in* and a person *out* of proper relationship with God.[9]

Indicative of this usage is the thought of Johann Arndt. Pietism appropriated much of its otherworldly language from this man whose writings had been so formative in the lives of young Spener and Francke. Arndt wrote of the Christian's contempt of the world as "a vale of tears, a place of misery, a deep dark prison."[10] But he also stressed biblical accents such as ". . . man was not created for the world's sake, but the world for man's."[11] He emphasized that the Scriptures employ the term "heart" to mean the whole man, body and soul.[12] He felt he was at one with Paul, who spoke not of two different parts of a person but of two opposing principles in the heart — the inward and the outward, the law of the mind and the law of the members, the spirit and the flesh.[13] Spener followed the Pauline emphasis in many of his own writings: "The body always should be a dwelling place of the Holy Spirit. Therefore, it is necessary that it at all times be treated moderately and purely, shunning all drunkenness and unchastity as vice, which God has banished. . . ."[14]

In this focus on the sacredness of the body and the goodness of creation, Pietism adopted a position of self-denial which denies pleasure in order to enhance creation and is motivated by desire for a greater good in this world. This is somewhat substantiated by a further examination of Spener's attitude toward adiaphora. This term was first applied to earlier controversies which surrounded the attempt to reintroduce Roman Catholic practices into Lutheranism by providing them with new meanings. Later the term was applied to the controversies involving moralistic restrictions. Literally, adiaphora are practices neither commanded nor forbidden by God and, consequently, are left to the choice of individuals. Throughout this debate which surrounded Pietism, Spener was inclined to deal leniently with those who believed they could safely enjoy many kinds of pleasure. He did not, for example, regard play as from the devil; it might even be conducive to health. He did not inordinately condemn either the dance or the theater; the latter, in fact, might even be used as the instrument of good.[15] His feeling about dancing came to be that it was not inherently wrong but subject to misuse and abuse. Spener's opposition to many of these diversions must be understood in the context of the ribaldry and debauchery of his times. He advised against them not because they were bad in themselves but because of their association with things much worse. He also felt that the days and weeks spent in preparation for festive occasions could have been more valuably employed in spiritual disciplines. The call of Jesus to self-denial should eliminate whatever action does not serve the honor of God or the spiritual welfare of our neighbors or ourselves.

For this reason, Spener advocated that pleasures of this nature be eliminated not so much by extreme condemnation as by the fostering of a spirit which lacked the desire for them. In this attitude Spener was more irenic than Francke, and some interpreters believe Francke's one-sided negative valuation of the world resulted more from his own personal disposition than from a false theology. In his defense of Francke's asceticism, Beyreuther claims that Francke had a legitimate reaction to the uninhibited eroticism of his day and a positive emphasis on the correct stewardship of time; only after his life did that asceticism become narrowly legalistic.[16]

End of the World

As seen in James Nichols' analysis of modern Christianity, it has often been assumed that Pietism's ascetical tendencies and devaluation of culture resulted from a chiliasm characterized by a despair of the world due to vivid expectations of the Second Coming of Christ: "He [Spener] had a strong expectation of the Second Coming, and his emphasis was on escape from a sinful world rather than its conquest."[17] That these caricatures are erroneous is obvious from an examination of Spener's position. Pietism's milieu did know a revival of eschatological speculations, but they were shaped into new forms. Spener treated this subject more extensively than Francke. His lifetime interest in eschatology stemmed from his doctoral dissertation, which involved an exegetical study of the passage beginning with Revelation 9:13. Through it, he became completely immersed in the world of apocalyptic and eschatological thought. His dissertation consisted of the compilation of forty commentaries into a table which compared the various views verse by verse. At the time he felt that he was more perplexed than enlightened by this research.[18] This initial irresolution concerning the details continued throughout his life. It blended with his hesitancy to offend in nonessentials, and, consequently, an exact explanation of his position is somewhat difficult. Nevertheless, he revealed enough that the main outlines of his beliefs can be discerned.

Spener developed a liberalized chiliasm and employed a non-literalistic exegesis. Unlike Bengel, he refused to become involved in setting dates, calling such activity "an encroachment on the secret counsels of God."[19] He believed that apocalyptic terms such as "heaven" and "paradise" are biblical expressions adapted to our childlike weaknesses. His more liberal views are seen in his comments referring to the more literalistic position of J. Petersen, his follower who held to the literal thousand-year reign of Christ:

> We cannot deny that this is Scriptural and that the early church held to it. Whether we should interpret it literally is another matter, although in most other cases we prefer this approach. For this reason we should not regard him as being foolish. It is an open question whether we should understand it as a precise thousand years as Petersen interprets or whether such a number indicates a round number, signifying a long time. Petersen interprets literally the chair, judgment, and reign. I am not as convinced as he. . . .[20]

In this and other passages, Spener revealed his rejection of premillennialism and the concept of double resurrection. But he did not relinquish his belief in a final judgment followed by either blessedness or damnation. Although doubts about the eternity of hell are natural, he felt that the scriptural evidence was too conclusive to believe otherwise.

In spite of the fact that Spener did not share Petersen's belief in the resurrection of the righteous prior to the millennium, he defended his friend by explaining that Article XVII of the Augsburg Confession was not directed against Petersen's brand of chiliasm but rather against that of the Anabaptists. The Anabaptists' proclamation of a holy kingdom in which believers judge the godless had been a real threat to the authority of government. Since Petersen completely repudiated the errors of the brand of Anabaptism here in mind, namely, the Münsterites, Spener felt that his teachings posed no threat to society and no basic deviation from the Symbolical Books. Consistent with his stance of toleration in nonessentials, Spener expressed the hope that Petersen would be allowed to continue in the ministry.[21]

Spener's own peculiar brand of chiliasm focused on a few specifics which were summarized when he characterized Pietists as "those who await in hope the fulfillment of the promise, which the church awaits, even the conversion of the Jews, the fall of Babel, and afterwards the glorious spread of the Kingdom of God."[22] From certain passages in the Book of Revelation and the eleventh chapter of Romans, Spener anticipated and proposed to work toward the conversion of the Jews and the final downfall of papal Rome, which he considered to be Babel, before the end of the world. Above all, he hoped for better times for the church. His optimism concerning the immanent power of the Spirit prompted him to regard pristine primitive Christianity as a historical possibility for the future.[23] He attempted to walk the middle road between a utopianism based on the hope for an actual earthly kingdom on the one hand and a despair of any improvement in the world on the other. Sectarian eschatology, for Spener, was to be taken seriously, if not literally.

This recurrent hope for better times and for the spread of the kingdom bequeathed to early Pietism a direction different than the one derived from world-negating re-

strictions. It also delivered Pietism from an exclusive stress
on individual salvation and ethics. The subsequent deliverance from subjectivism is stated ably by Dorner in his
discussion of eschatology:

> Hence it was but in accordance with the normal relation
> of things that Spener — the very man who so greatly con-
> tributed to the re-animation of the evangelical principle of
> faith, and exhorted men with such peculiar earnestness to
> care for the salvation of their own souls — should, when the
> time was come, burst in an unexpected manner the bonds
> of spurious subjectiveness, . . . and direct the hope of be-
> lievers to the grand historical development of a *future* king-
> dom.[24]

According to this thesis, the eschatological emphases are
productive of rather than antithetical to ethical concerns.
Eschatology is transformed into history, and through this
transformation it becomes more than a doctrine of the last
things. Such a reversal stamps a new significance on history
as the sphere in which God is contemporarily at work. The
emphasis on *Heilsgeschichte* ("history of salvation") ac-
knowledges this debt to Spener's thought. Contrary to the
analysis that Spener's eschatology was escapist, it was
his hope for better times which gave the Protestant church
of the second century following the Reformation the conviction that Christianity had been preserved through the
struggle of the Thirty Years' War for the purpose of ful-
filling a mission to the world. Spener believed the eschatological hope must become a present reality: the kingdom,
which will be completely realized only in the future, must
begin to penetrate present history through the renewal of
the church, evangelistic endeavors, and various philanthropic and social missions.[25]

Mission to the World

There is probably nothing in which historians have been more unfair to Pietism than in defining the mission of the church to society. A frequent stereotype of Pietistic Christianity portrays it as almost exclusively preoccupied with inward devotion and private moral scruples. On the contrary, the Pietist milieu resulted in a desire to transform the living conditions of the poor and oppressed, reform the prison system, abolish slavery, break down rigid class distinctions, establish a more democratic polity, initiate educational reforms, establish philanthropic institutions, increase missionary activity, obtain religious liberty, and propose programs for social justice. But were these merely the by-products of a gospel which was essentially personal and an ethic which was individualistic? It is true that Pietistic lifestyles led to a sharp decline in drunkenness and adultery among clergy and laity. Though not consciously intended, Pietism produced indirect by-products such as the strengthening of the new *Bürger* class in German society, the fostering of the necessary ambition and purpose to recover from the devastating Thirty Years' War, and the nurturing of Enlightenment humanism. Even among movements concerned only about personal spiritual growth and salvation, class barriers are transcended in lives reflecting the transforming power of the message. For example, at Halle the treatment of the poor and orphans as educable was in itself socially transforming.

Analysts influenced by Marxist notions have seen in Pietism another expression of otherworldliness and devotional preoccupation which serves as an "opiate of the people," keeping them from awareness of political exploitation and social injustice. It has likewise been argued that Pietists have been the unwitting instruments of class conflict, as in the struggle in Prussia of the developing middle class and bureaucratic absolutism against the traditional autonomy of the feudal nobility and their control over the peasants in the nineteenth century.[26] A few years ago a favorite slogan emerged among secular theologians: "From Pietism to Servanthood." It appeared to be a call from preoccupation with private ethics to participation in social structures.

Though containing some elements of truth, most such historical analyses do not stand the test of closer scrutiny. Concerning the "opiate" label, such reasoning would be more applicable to Lutheran Orthodoxy than to Pietism. Luther's doctrine of two kingdoms was interpreted by the latter in such a way as to mitigate against any direct influence of the church over the secular structures. A closer examination of the struggle in Prussia reveals that early Pietists took part as churchmen in political decisions of the time. And the examination of Pietist writings and institutional expressions demonstrates that the Pietist servant-hood theme was basic from the beginning.

Though most of the otherworldly and individualistic charges might more appropriately be directed to Lutheran Orthodoxy, it can be granted that due to its Lutheran matrix, early Pietism did not begin to approximate the social gospel movement of modern times. However, there is evidence of greater direct social concern than is commonly attributed. So much concern, in fact, that Pietism probably contained the seeds for the prophetic kingdom theology of the Blumhardts in the nineteenth century and for the impetus which helped produce later social prophets such as Walter Rauschenbusch.

In his *Pia Desideria*, Spener criticized some businesses, professions, economic practices, and public ordinances as opposed to the commandments of Christ. He deplored the fact that the expediency of selfish acquisition was often exalted above the good of neighbor and the glory of God, a phrase which we have come to see as basic to Pietist nomenclature.[27] Community of goods, however, should not be regarded as a legalistic necessity. Instead, love demands that one must give up possessions for the needs of fellow servants freely and not because they demand such a worldly right. Spener admired the early communism of the church. "To early Christians neither complete community of goods or worldly ownership became a hindrance to brotherly love. Thus among them the rich had no advantages over others, since they also had to be rich in good works."[28] He deplored not only the fact that his church fell so far short of the New Testament pattern but also that love was not even as much in evidence in his day as in the Old Testament, in which we discover that frequently a tenth was given to support priestly services and to aid the poor.[29] Though it is often assumed that Spener's thought gave rise to a basis for philanthropy rather than a program designed to change the structure of institutions, there is evidence to the contrary. Spener worked effectively in Frankfurt and Berlin to establish welfare programs for those who were still suffering from the tragic economic effects of the Thirty Years' War.[30] He emphasized the necessity of such help without causing a loss of self-respect on the part of the recipients. Such active concern with social reform legislation was indicative of a transformationist ethic which was undoubtedly influenced by his Calvinist contacts in Strasbourg and Geneva and which represented a clear departure from Luther's two-kingdom doctrine.

Francke saw in his institutions a means to individual and community improvement. He believed his educational enterprises would help reduce "Theft, Robbery, and other such heinous Crimes."[31] He was confident that his orphans would prove to be useful servants, "promoting the Good and Advantage whether of Church or State."[32] In presenting the purposes of the Widows' Home, Francke reveals a real measure of concern for the world. "The real design of this Foundation is not only to maintain these poor Widows when broken with Age, but to withal instruct them how they ought to pray for the Welfare of the City, of the whole Country, of our Sovereign, and the whole Catholick Church."[33] Beyreuther writes extensively of Francke's great sense of social responsibility. He summarizes Francke's views in one sentence: "Conversion and regeneration should lead man into service on behalf of the social betterment of the world."[34] When Frederick Wilhelm I visited Francke in Halle in 1713, he asked, "What do you think of war?" Although not a pacifist, Francke answered, "Your majesty must defend the land, but I am called to preach, 'Blessed are the peacemakers.' "[35] Though such a comment can easily be subsumed in a two-kingdom theology, Francke and Spener were much more critical against the folly of warfare and more active in programs of reconciliation than was usual for their time.

Pietism did not spawn "Holy Commonwealths" as readily as Puritanism. The Pietist expression has focused less on the legislation of morality for all and more on each individual's adoption of a Christian lifestyle. Though Luther's doctrine of the two spheres had resulted in a somewhat docile Pietist posture toward the state, there was nevertheless a surprising degree of resistance to the caesaropapism of that day. Spener and Francke were often bold in their utterances to the governmental authorities. Spener's belief in religious freedom resulted from his conviction that a ruler has the power to rule over earthly things and the external person only; conscience and the inner person remain free, and the ruler has no power over them. When rulers attempt to gain authority over the inner person, the subjects are not bound to obey.[36] Spener attempted to follow his own advice, obediently submitting to the authorities in most instances, yet proclaiming modest remonstrations when necessary.[37] Francke, who preached against the fear of man and appealed for Christian boldness, was exemplary of his own message. It is reported that after he preached in the presence of the king, the ruler said, "Francke is a good man. He speaks the truth to every one."[38] In addition to religious freedom and a more prophetic stance toward governmental rulers, the Pietists abetted democratization by renewing emphasis on the priesthood of all believers and opposing caesaropapism. The vital influence of Pietism among the nobility in many areas led to more benevolent rule and support of humanitarian enterprises.

It would be fallacious to attempt to deny all otherworldly elements in Pietism. It would also be wrong to try to equate the social strategy of the early Pietists with later transformationist, social gospel, or liberation theologies. Nevertheless, Pietism did represent a greater social concern than its Lutheran genesis, and many common caricatures of Pietism are lacking in total perspective. The asceticism of their moralistic rules was mollified by zealous participation in philanthropic and missionary activities. Their general devaluation of culture was greatly modified by an eschatology which focused on this world. The Pietist reaction against worldliness was due to a revulsion against the excesses of the times; yet the otherworldly feeling against bad times was transformed into a desire for a reformed church in this world. While the emphasis on service did not include all of the elements of the sophisticated political theology of more recent years, it did intend for holiness to be lived out in the world. For these reasons, more positive evaluations concerning Pietism's social stance have been appearing. Brunner credited Pietism's social amelioration and foreign missions with being "among the most splendid records of achievement to be found in Church history."[39] And Tillich wrote of Pietism's "great influence on culture as a whole."[40]

VII

A Contemporary Critique

Up to this point I have tried to be as objective as possible in examining and interpreting a greatly misunderstood movement; yet my efforts have been unavoidably limited by a sympathetic bias nurtured by my own background in the Church of the Brethren, which traces a side of its origins to the Pietist milieu. Most German scholarly work on this subject has not been by those who identify personally with the Pietist label. It is truly amazing that a scholar such as the nineteenth-century historian Albrecht Ritschl would expend such massive efforts to produce a detailed three-volume history of a movement about which he cared so little.[1] It may be time for some of America's Pietistic stepchildren to endeavor to achieve some balance in Pietist historiography.[2]

I believe that it is fairer to first interpret a movement in the light of its origin rather than of its later manifestations. In attempting to do for Pietism what has been done for other movements such as Lutheranism and Methodism, we have turned to the foremost of the churchly Pietists, Spener and Francke. We have seen how they professed a mediating position between dogmatic rigidity and emotional warmth, faith and works, law and gospel, justification and sanctification, judgment and love of the world. They desired a corrective rather than a revolutionary movement. Reformation rather than separation constituted their ecclesiastical goal, though they often empathized with a Radical Pietist mood which considered the church to be Babel. From my perspective, some of their weaknesses were offset by basic strengths. In relation to the Bible, for example, the perils of private interpretation must be viewed in light of increased usage, study, and exegesis. The devaluation of culture must be judged in the perspective of a this-worldly eschatology in which the future kingdom must begin to become a present reality. Its ascetic tendencies must be balanced by the notable missionary and philanthropic endeavors. Its experiential existentialism must be examined in the context of a doctrine of the Holy Spirit in which the Bible, sacraments, and the church were the means for appropriating Spirit, Word, and the work of God. Even today, the theology of Spener and Francke offers an ecumenical appeal in balance and irenic spirit.

Nevertheless, corrective movements, even those which strive to be mediating, need to be corrected themselves. Another side of my theology and tradition does not identify with Pietism, and consequently I have often found in the early movement the seeds of later degenerations and errors. This has frequently evoked in me an ambivalent attitude toward "pietistic manifestations." The group movement is a case in point. Because of my identity with the idea of conventicles, I have often gravitated to cell groups, prayer groups, house churches, T-groups, D-groups, sensitivity groups, and encounter groups. But because of my historical knowledge of potential degenerations, anxiety often surfaces more quickly in me than in others when I sense an excessive preoccupation with a subjectivity which ignores input from outside (in Christian terms, the Word of God), and fails to display any sense of compassion or mission for the world beyond the group. Such a dialectical attitude toward the group movement may well be a paradigm of my perspective toward basic issues related to Pietism.

The Question of Mini-Ethics

As orthodox Christians have been accused of making a Christ of truth instead of beholding the truth in Christ, so Pietists have often made a god of goodness instead of discerning the goodness of God. Pietism was right, I believe, in accenting the ethical nature of the Christian faith. As the juridical metaphor, justification, focuses on God making things right with us, the biological metaphor, regeneration, points to the new creation in which barriers are eliminated between male and female, slave and free, Jew and Gentile. One cannot separate the two greatest commandments — our love for God and our love for others — from each other. Pietists rightly echoed the Johannine claim that if we say we love God and hate our sisters and brothers, we are liars. Pietists at their best have assumed the Judeo-Christian tradition to be fundamentally ethical.

Pietism was wrong in often regarding a pattern of goodness as normative to the faith instead of seeing goodness as the fruit of faith. The danger of legalism lurks in the valid emphasis that Christianity is to be viewed as all of life; the Christian life can falsely become defined as a set of rules. I find in the early movement the seeds of a persisting phenomenon of Pietism, namely, the reduction of

Christianity to mini-ethics, in which the essence of discipleship is reduced to a few do's and don't's. Don't smoke, drink, dance, or gamble. Do attend church regularly, pay your tithes, and pray before meals. Such rules can easily evolve into a works theology in which one neglects the weightier issues of love and justice.

I have attempted to point out both the validity and dangers of such personal disciplines by placing them within the framework of a theology of symbolism. Non-smoking, for example, might serve as a symbol which in Tillich's language points beyond itself at the same time it participates in that to which it points. Symbolically, non-smoking can point to the theological affirmations of the application of religion to all of life, the Hebraic unity of spirit and body, and a valid nonconformity to the manipulative and brainwashing aspects of modern culture. Insofar as this helps move us toward a genuine concern for all of God's creation and helps us to be nonconformists in reference to more vital issues, then such a symbol not only points beyond itself but genuinely participates in that to which it points. But when rules such as the one against smoking become the essence of Christianity, the test of church membership, or a means of evaluating character, then we have become idolatrous. We have worshiped the symbol, in this case a non-biblical symbol, instead of using it to point to the realities of our faith. In many respects the various brands of situational ethics and the new morality may represent a deserved judgment on our propensities to love rules and hate people. But in order to repudiate legalism, it is not necessary that we become antinomian.

In order to transcend such preoccupation with mini-ethics, we can learn from both the failures and successes of the early Pietist movement. We live in a time which knows a new clamor to close the gap between word and deed. Many of our younger contemporaries have not so much been interested in new theologies as in putting the old ones into practice. Inasmuch as the early Pietist emphasis on sanctification was formulated with a radical eschatology, in which Spener expected better times for the church and some of the Radical Pietists were looking for a seventh age of peace, we need to participate again in a union of eschatology and ethics. An ethic of promise can redefine the absolute. The absolute ethic is not so much a code which has been decreed from the past as a promise of what shall be in the future. It is not a prescription that tells us what we have to be; it is a description of a challenge to what we can and shall become. Since such perfection is in the future, there will be no claims of attainment. Thus there is no room for pride and self-righteousness. The kingdom ethics are absolute in the sense that they challenge us to begin to live now as if the kingdom has already come. Our optimism, then, need not be based on views of natural goodness as much as on the possibility of grace arriving through persons. It is precisely this Pietist emphasis on sanctification or goodness from God which needs to be revived in our time.

The Peril of Individualism

Luther's accent on personal pronouns was intensified in Pietist circles. Since the Christian faith focuses on a Person as the clue to reality rather than on books, philosophical truths, a set of rules, or inner discovery, the Christian legacy includes the emphasis on the personal. Each person is of supreme worth in the eyes of God. Personal decision is important. These themes were rightly highlighted in Pietism. Nevertheless, early and later Pietism often erred in translating as singular the plural pronouns of the Bible. In Pietistic hymnody and life, "our Father" too often becomes "my father." Christ died for me rather than for us, Israel, or the world. So many Pietist, holiness, pentecostal, fundamental, and revival hymnbooks are really not biblical in their choice of pronouns. From the beginning of the Pietist movement this individualization began to corrupt basic doctrines dealing with the theology of experience, of salvation, and of conversion.

Christ

In some circles there developed an almost exclusive preoccupation with a relationship to Christ as "personal Savior," a phrase difficult to find in the New Testament, though the idea might be deduced from the total message. This undermined what is found more explicitly in the biblical passages, namely, the declaration that Christ is Savior of the world and of Israel. Pietists have often been accused of wanting to be alone with Jesus in the garden in order to keep him there and prevent him from being Lord of all of life. The basis for such tendencies can be found in the sermons and literature of early Pietists such as Zinzendorf and Francke. With the rightful emphasis on personal decision must be incorporated the message that we decide for a cosmic Christ; for God "has put all things under his feet and has made him the head over all things for the church" (Ephesians 1:22). A friend of mine once commented that a particular group of people had a higher Christology than others. Knowing there were liberals among them, I objected. He retorted that their Christology was high because they were willing to let Christ be Lord over more areas of their lives. Christology is certainly determined by what one affirms about Christ. But Pietist theology at its best should also evaluate one's faith according to how little or how much Christ is allowed to be Lord over the many areas of life. Since in Christ our personal salvation can never be separated from our relationships with others, salvation becomes personal only through our personal response to the social dimensions of the faith, which includes God and neighbor.

Holy Spirit

One biblical meaning of the Holy Spirit has been that the Third Person of the Trinity is God in action. The biblical metaphors of wind, power, and fire reveal that God is at work in the world in general and special ways. Insisting that though we cannot be saved by works, faith must nevertheless become active in love, the Pietists similarly stressed that though we cannot be saved through experience alone, faith must nevertheless show in the totality of life, in joy and in emotions. This intensification of faith, this stress that the power of the early Christians can be ours as well, and all of the testimonies of warmed hearts and great joy have been the great strength as well as one of the potential dangers of Pietism. It is precisely this phenomenon which Eldridge Cleaver believes the blacks to have taught the whites through the civil rights struggles of the sixties, namely, the tapping of the emotional dimensions of our existence. We can call it soul. We might label it historically as Pietism. In biblical circles it has been named as the Hebraic or holistic response of the person to God.

Another biblical dimension of the Spirit is that given by Paul in 2 Corinthians 3:17: "The Lord is the Spirit. . . ." Pietists have frequently identified the working of the Spirit with dreams, visions, voices, special revelations, and specific answers to prayer. We have seen how Spener, who did not deny such manifestations, did maintain that they must be tested by the Spirit of Christ. My own reaction to all who see halos, talk with their departed loved ones, or display psychic gifts such as ESP communication is one of granting that such phenomena may well exist. Who am I to deny possible valid discoveries in parapsychology? As a Christian, however, I propose that all such activity must be tested by the Spirit of Christ. Does it measure up to the loving Spirit of Jesus or is it basically a representation of our own selfish wishes and purposes? Such a test of whether a phenomenon is "for others" or "according to the will of God as we know it in Christ" is one which can deliver pietists and charismatics today from the perils of individualism. In seeking deliverance from such self-centered motivation, the help and guidance of others in Christ is indispensable.

A third biblical connotation of the Holy Spirit, I believe, may be expressed by the phrase "the community of the Spirit." In the New Testament and Christian tradition there has been an intimate connection between powerful manifestations of the Spirit of God and the community of faith. Pentecost conjoined a time of special outpouring of the Holy Spirit with the birthday of the Christian church. In the story of the preaching of Philip in Acts 8 and the story of the vision of Paul on the Damascus road, we meet the teaching that the Holy Spirit does not come fully until the laying on of hands by representatives of the church. Here is a corporate emphasis in conversion which has too often been ignored in pietistic circles. Here is the biblical truth that the Holy Spirit comes to us through the life of the community of faith, through the lives of other Christians. We do not just become converted and then join others who have had similar experiences; rather, relationships with others are a part of God's converting action.

Salvation

Unfortunately, salvation and shalom have often been defined in pietist circles almost exclusively in terms of personal salvation and peace of soul. In this way the salvation story has been presented as an escape from this sinful world rather than as a salvation from self in order to live for God and for others. Life is compartmentalized into the sacred and the secular. To attain personal peace and to escape the problems of the world and have a good feeling in church are viewed as the essence of practicing Christianity. This has often led pietists to make an easy peace with the world in the social sphere because the social and political spheres are wicked anyway and have nothing to do with Christianity. It was Bonhoeffer who polemicized against this tendency to translate Christianity into a mystery or salvation cult instead of into a religion of historical redemption.

In reality, shalom, which is the Hebraic biblical synonym for salvation, knows a far richer meaning. It is at once salvation, peace, integrity, community, harmony, wholeness, health, social righteousness, justice, and right relationships. Likewise, the concept of the soul is broader biblically than has sometimes been found in Pietist usage. Early Pietist writings connote that the soul dwells in the heart, the good part of the person, rather than in the bad part, called the body. But we have also seen that the total thought of early Pietism is more complex. Instead of referring to a good part of each of us, many references to the soul and heart point to singleness of purpose, purity of motive, and wholeness of personality. The soul is not a separate part located in a separate place but is the whole person in or out of right relationship with God. If the soul were only good, then it would not need saving. Many of us have encountered a frequent rhetorical question: "Why doesn't the church stick to its business of saving souls?" In response we can express our agreement with the concern while at the same time we indicate our disagreement with what is implied concerning the meaning of salvation. For if the soul is the whole person and salvation is God's bringing this person into proper relationships with himself and others, then we can reply, "Yes, the church must stick to the business of saving souls, but to save souls is to engage in any activity which brings people in whole relationships with one another and their Creator." In expanding the biblical doctrine of salvation this broadly, we do not eliminate the necessity of each Christian making a strong personal commitment to this mission and its Lord. The early Pietist fathers represented two types in relation to conversion. Spener, who remembered that he had always been a good boy, did not experience a dramatic conversion experience. Such was not the case with Francke, who knew adolescent waywardness, crisis, and intense doubt. Though it is debated how much he expected the same of others, it was Francke who bequeathed to Pietism the penitential struggle and dated conversion experience. Pietists have been right in preaching and expecting radical conversion but have often been wrong in expecting all people to have the same experience in the same way. Though it is commendable when we can testify to the working of God in our lives, it is wrong to limit the coming of the Spirit to one style. The New Testament teaches the necessity of the new birth but leaves it up to the Holy Spirit to fill in the details as to time, place, and method. As pietists should avoid legalizing the fruit of faith into absolute codes of conduct, so they must beware of schematizing the experience of faith into normative steps on the road to salvation.

Pietism has likewise often degenerated into a theology of personal success in which peace of mind, physical health, and worldly success are promised as a result of an active faith. This is the temptation of some faith healing, Jesus, and charismatic movements today. One finds the seeds of this in Francke. When his institutions were greatly in need of help, his circle prayed fervently. As gifts followed, there was a strong emphasis on the offering of thanksgiving to God in response to another glorious manifestation of his providence. Some of his followers, past and present, have so perverted this emphasis as to violate the biblical injunction "that whoever would save his life will lose it" (Matthew 10:39). We are to seek first the kingdom, not our own welfare. We are to pray that God's will, not ours, be done. Only then should we rejoice in personal and material blessings which may be ours as well.

The Issue of Reformism

Generally, pietist strategy has been that of changing society through changed individuals. Such evolutionary penetration of the structures of society differs from a Puritan mood which adds to the results of conversion an attempt to legislate morality for the entire commonwealth. Sobriety and personal abstinence are fruits of Pietism, for example, while Puritanism can more logically add to these the concern for prohibition. The strategies through the years, however, have become jumbled. This is illustrated in the way that some of the same people who maintain that racism can never be successfully attacked through law but only through changed hearts advocate strict laws in reference to drinking. On the other hand, those who lay the primary stress on the individual rehabilitation of alcoholics are frequently those who advocate laws for civil rights.

The pietist strategy is commendable in its insistence that Christians should first practice for themselves what is preached for the world. Change comes basically through example and persuasion rather than through law and coercion. As a result of the emphasis on the love of God and neighbor, pietistic compassion highlighted the servant role.

From the orphanage and widows' homes at Halle to the extensive activities of the *Innere Mission* philanthropic activity of the last century, Pietism has attempted to be faithful to the biblical admonitions to give alms, share the cup of cold water, and show concern for the poor. More recently the servant role has been under attack because it has often helped to make life just tolerable enough to divert the oppressed from challenging their bad situation. Likewise, such charity often represents a paternalism in which giving relieves misery only slightly and is manipulated to encourage persons to conform to the middle-class value systems of the benefactors. Because of the nature of much so-called Christian service, the critique has especially opposed a Band-Aid approach which tries to patch up the devastating effects of injustice instead of getting at the root causes of our social maladies. In spite of the validity of these charges, we can continue to affirm some pietist-like service ministries. Those who put on Band-Aids are likely to be moved to seek out the sources of infection. In fact, many who have sympathetically identified with the oppressed through a servant role have become the ones who are most existentially involved in the attacks on injustice.

Nevertheless, the insistence on working through the present structures for gradual change, though always an option to be taken seriously, is not an adequate Christian social strategy in itself. It does not consider seriously enough our corporate sinfulness. Concerning individual conversion, the Pietists regarded sin so seriously as to maintain that the cure could only be found beyond the person in God's revelation and action. If Pietists should regard the sins we commit together with equal seriousness, there would be a realization that salvation will not always come through natural evolution, the hope of reformism, or through the penetration of structures by Christian activists. Something other may be needed. The sick structures may be saved only by something external — the apocalyptic vision of God's pulling humanity to live in the new age of the kingdom, the forming of new communities of persons who are being liberated from and for the fallen institutions of the present age.

The more evolutionary mood of Pietism probably needs a greater dosage of biblical apocalypticism. By this I do not mean an apocalypticism which places the kingdom entirely in the future or one which moves it entirely outside history. Instead, I am referring to what I regard to be the New Testament version which knows a radical disjunction between the present age and the age to come but which expects the coming kingdom to break into the present. The kingdom hope comes not from our achievements but from God's activity through us. The proclamation that the kingdom is at hand does not just mean that individuals are being saved but involves sharing through word and deed the way of righteousness, justice, and peace. The Christian mandate calls for more than the participation of saved individuals in the structures of society. The church is called to proclaim corporately a message to individuals and to the corporate structures, the powers and principalities. It may be too much to expect the fallen world to easily adopt this way; nevertheless, we are called to preach the gospel to all, including those in positions of power. We are called to witness to persons both in their individual situations and their corporate life.

Recently, I have been refusing to make normative either the traditional Pietist option of working within structures or the Radical Pietist and sectarian option of serving outside in possible counter-structures. The important criterion is faithfulness. In some periods of history and in some instances for each of us, faithfulness will mean that we serve within the present structures as God's servants for renewal and reformation. In other instances it may be God's will for us to shake the dust off our feet and leave the present structures in order to witness and serve God's kingdom through new ones. The only justification for leaving structures is to serve in new ways. For example, if some are called to leave the present institutionalized forms of the church, the call should be to become the church in a new way. Whether inside or outside present structures, the pietist mood would have us attempt to keep in dialogue with one another. For the pietist genius, gradualism, tolerance, and reconciliation must be contributed to and corrected by a more bold prophetic stance toward the powers that be.

The Legacy of Pietism

In our theological critique of Pietism we have focused primarily on the thought of the earliest leaders. But we frequently have discovered in their theology the seed of later degenerations. In addition to its positive influence, every historical analysis should grant that Pietism has contributed to hypocritical legalism, experiential fanaticism, narrow-minded dogmatism, and loveless separatism. Nevertheless, there have been many who have credited or discredited the movement with too much. For example, historian Koppel S. Pinson wrote an entire book to demonstrate that the enthusiasm of Pietism provided the emotional base for subsequent German nationalism.[3] Though it is true that Pietism contributed to the increased use of the vernacular and that Fichte employed the word *"Wiedergeburt"* for the German nation, Pinson too easily identified Pietism with emotionalism and overlooked the international flavor of the early movement.

Though any critique of Pietism must attempt to examine the merits and demerits of early thought and later manifestations, an acknowledgment of its multifaceted legacy is essential. Paul Tillich's aforementioned judgment of Pietism's great influence on culture can be documented. Though our data will be incomplete and necessarily abbreviated, I offer a sweeping recital of its many influences in order again to make the case that we are dealing with an important historical phenomenon in the history of western Christianity, a phenomenon which has received so little attention from English and American historians.

Philosophically, the *Aufklärung* ("German Enlightenment") has often been regarded as the product of Pietism because of the easy transition from the belief in the Spirit as the autonomous guide for life to the rational guidance which everyone has by the possession of reason. It is reported that John Salomo Sempler, the rationalist, conducted family devotions with much fervor. Troeltsch wrote a book about Leibniz and his relationship to Pietism.[4] According to Martin Schmidt, "Lessing is unthinkable without spiritualism and Pietism."[5] It was a common saying in the eighteenth century that "he who goes to Halle returns either a Pietist or a Rationalist."[6] Among German universities, Halle was the first to yield to rationalism. Nevertheless, there were fundamental differences between Pietism and the Enlightenment in the views of original sin, revelation, the source of piety, and the Bible. We must also keep in mind the possibility that the extreme intellectualism of late Orthodoxy may have likewise contributed to the coming of the Age of Reason. To deny direct causative relationships because of fundamental differences is not to deny, however, that indirectly Pietism helped prepare the way for the German Enlightenment. Both emerged from the misery of the period following 1648. Both constituted reactions to the clerical, legalistic, and institutional Christianity of the day. Both shared the accents of individualism and religious freedom, and the view that life is to be changed in a practical way. Primarily, it was the focus on life and ethics in an atmosphere of tolerance which did the most to prepare the way for the dogmatic indifference of the Enlightenment and the pluralism of modern times.

The experiential and moral dimensions of Pietism are often cited as sources of later German romanticism and idealism. Kant, Schiller, Fichte, Novalis, and Goethe in part were educated along Pietistic lines. Immanuel Kant often eulogized the beauty of his home life with Pietist parents. His mother was an admirer of pastor F. A. Schultz, who had been a student of Francke. It was Schultz who guided the young Kant to a high school of the Halle vintage. Although Kant soon developed an antipathy for the stilted piety, hypocrisy, and somber discipline of his surroundings, he retained a deep sense of the radical evil of human nature, the stringency of the ethical, and the categorical imperative to duty.

Theologically, largely due to its theology of religious experience, Pietism has been named a root of both Fundamentalism and Liberalism. The doctrines of conversion, regeneration, and holiness of life were carried into the many awakenings and revivals of the eighteenth and nineteenth centuries. Through theologians like Friedrich Schleiermacher, who once referred to himself as a "Pietist of a higher order," this same empiricism was formative in the epistemology of Liberalism. We have already seen how the hermeneutics of Pietism led to both the *Heilsgeschichte* ("history of salvation") and dispensationalist strands in biblical circles. An integral part of this legacy has been the reminder of the necessity and possibility of emulating original Christianity in the present era. Ruth Rouse and Stephen Neill featured the unionist efforts and international context of Pietism in their treatment of the origins of the ecumenical movement.[7] In contrast to the Reformation and Pietist Radicals and to mystical spiritualism, Pietism prevented the rise of a Christianity outside the church through its emphasis on reformism through the conventicles.

Accompanying these philosophical and theological currents were the wide geographical spread and institutional concretions of the Pietist movement. Halle with its many institutions provided the axis for the influence of early Pietism. Of Francke and his work, the American Puritan Cotton Mather observed: "The World begins to feel a Warmth from the *Fire of God*, which thus flames in the heart of *Germany*, beginning to extend into many Regions;

the whole world will ere long be sensible of it."[8] When Frederick IV of Denmark wished to send missionaries to his foreign colonies, he turned to Halle to find them. Ziegenbalg and Plütschau, who were appointed by Francke and journeyed to Tranquebar, India, as missionaries in 1706, were the first of many to be sent from this center. The consequent need for the translation and printing of Bibles and other devotional materials was filled by the Halle-based Canstein Bible Institute.

Halle Pietism spread early to Scandinavia. An interesting development occurred in 1713 when Francke began to send money, hymnbooks, tracts, and Bibles to Swedish prisoners in Siberia. Enjoying a great amount of freedom from the Russians, the exiles established schools after the Halle pattern. A pietistic awakening resulted among the prisoners. The Russians became interested, and Peter the Great requested teachers from Prussia. After the demise of absolutism with the death of Charles XII in 1718, Pietism penetrated quickly into Sweden through the returned soldiers from Siberia and students from the German universities. Pietism sunk even deeper roots in Finland where, along with Norway, pietistic flavor has been retained to this day.

Pietism was also carried by immigrants.[9] The first major German migration to the New World in 1683 was allied with Pietism. Following Penn's second visit to Germany in 1677, Franz Pastorius and other members of Spener's conventicle in Frankfurt formed the Frankfurt Land Company, which purchased 25,000 acres of land, the site of the future Germantown in Pennsylvania. The father of American Lutheranism, Heinrich Mühlenberg, was sent by

Francke's son to America in response to a plea for leadership. A disciple of Spener, Mühlenberg reported regularly to Halle and turned to its personnel for additional ministers for the American frontier. Another Halle student, Anton Boehm, was appointed in 1705 to be a preacher in the court of Prince George in England. He was instrumental in translating many Pietist devotional materials into English, and along with Isaac Watts served as a liaison between German Pietism and English and American Puritanism.

Francke's institutions became exemplary for philanthropic endeavors in other places. His own account of his work was translated into English under the title *Pietas Hallensis* and was widely circulated in the English-speaking world. It was appended to Whitefield's *Orphan-House,* an account of a similar enterprise in Georgia. Of even greater interest to historians have been the pedagogical principles operative in these institutions. Francke's innovations are often regarded by historians of educational philosophy as seminal to later developments. His primary principle was the education of the will. The example of the teacher was considered very important. In his schools students and teachers lived together, a radical innovation for his place and time. An educational pragmatist, Francke stressed training in trades for those without the aptitude to advance academically. He was one of the first to become interested in providing education for girls. He is considered by many to be the father of the elementary school system of Germany. Rejecting the more common beatings and discipline resulting from a sudden loss of temper, he nevertheless maintained strong discipline and close supervision of the children.

The early influences of Pietism are not to be limited exclusively to Halle. Spenerian emphases became a vital part of the church life of Germany. Pastoral visitation, increased hymnological activity, and better preaching were in evidence in many areas. The reformation practices of catechetical instruction and public confirmations were revived. Lay responsibility and lay participation received new impetus. It was in Württemberg that Pietism was to have its most permanent influence. In southern Germany, it became more of a people's movement. The *Stunden*, which were prayer meetings, sought to combat separatism by emphasizing attendance at worship and participation in the sacraments. To this day Württemberg knows *Stunden* and retains a Pietistic atmosphere.

Some of the early developments led to established denominations. Though historians have vacillated in their judgments concerning the relative weight of Pietist influence, the following listing should be illustrative of the significance of the legacy of Pietism in ecclesiastical movements. One of the most contemporaneous with Spener and Francke was the community of faith which originated at Schwarzenau in Wittgenstein in 1708, which was known as *Täufer* ("Baptists") or *Neutäufer* ("New Baptist" in contrast with the Old Baptists, Anabaptists) and which is presently known as the Church of the Brethren. Brethren historiography has focused on the relative weight to be placed on the Pietist heritage as compared to the Anabaptist. Both have been stressed, along with the rootage in the Reformed and Lutheran traditions. Donald Durnbaugh, who is recognized as the most knowledgeable of Brethren historians, judges that the early Brethren came out of and rejected their Radical Pietist stance in more consciously identifying with Anabaptism.[10] Their formation of a church constituted in itself a repudiation of Radical Pietist theology. Nevertheless, all Brethren historians agree that the early Brethren retained from the Pietist milieu a quality of zeal, a suspicion of creeds, the doctrine of universal restoration, and an emphasis on the experiential appropriation of the Holy Spirit.

Sharing to an even greater extent the spirit of Radical Pietism was another movement which had its origin in the same Schwarzenau locale. The Community of True Inspiration, or Inspirationists, stemmed from a few French Huguenots who fled from France to Germany following the revocation of the Edict of Nantes. They were joined by deflectors from Württemberg Pietism. They believed that God would reveal himself in extraordinary revelations to special prophets to be held in equal esteem with the Bible. Coming to New York State in 1842, the community later moved to Iowa, where they became best known as the Amana colonies. Only within the last decades has their communal ownership of goods been gradually abandoned.

More closely related to the mainstream of Pietism than either of the above two movements was Moravianism. Count Nicolaus Ludwig von Zinzendorf (1700-60) was cradled in Pietism. A godson of Spener, tutored, privileged, and devout, Zinzendorf was sent to Francke's *Pädagogium* from the ages of ten to seventeen. In 1722, remnants of the pre-Reformation Bohemian Brethren settled on his estate and founded Herrnhut, "the Lord's watch." Following a revival under his leadership, the Count resigned his post to settle among the Brethren. On May 12, 1727, a political-churchly community with its own constitution and worship services was created. The piety was more emotional and sentimental than at Halle, and the struggle for repentance was replaced by a more joyful and personal relationship with the Savior. The leader's ecumenical spirit led his followers to regard themselves as a movement within Lutheranism rather than as a separate denomination (as later evolved in America and elsewhere). Early Moravianism possessed rich liturgy and music, evangelistic zeal, worldwide missionary activity, and an exemplary brotherhood. Its impact on the eighteenth century was dynamic, and its influence was felt by many, including the Wesley brothers in England.

The Moravians' most direct influence on the Wesleys occurred during the three troublesome years which antedated John Wesley's conversion. On board the ship *Simmonds*, sailing to America, Wesley was deeply impressed with the calmness and faith of the Moravians during a terrible storm. As a young priest in Georgia, Wesley had almost daily contacts with the Moravian colonists. Upon return to England, young Peter Böhler, along with the Moravian-inspired societies, formed the matrix for the conversion of the two famous brothers and the renowned Aldersgate experience in 1738. Pietism and Methodism shared a revived emphasis on conversion, charismatic power, sanctification, and reform through small groups within the life of the church. Following his pilgrimage to the cradle of Pietism at Herrnhut and Halle, however, Wesley broke with the Moravians because of what he called their anti-nomianism and quietism and because of the authoritarianism of the Count. The Great Awakening in America, like its Wesleyan English counterparts, has been identified as another wave of Pietism. Though it is more accurate to label these later movements with more precise historical designations, German Pietism and its literature were no doubt influential in the revivals. This is seen in the frequent affirmations of the Pietist nature of the ministry of Jonathan Edwards. William Warren Sweet, for example, explains Edwardianism as the impregnation of Calvinism with Pietism.[11]

The influence of Pietism was not limited to new movements and revivals; its impact was also felt on older movements. Harold Bender, the dean of Anabaptist scholars, observed that Pietism in some form or other has been the most powerful modifying influence on the Mennonites since the sixteenth century.[12] In the later revivals of the nineteenth century, pietistic currents spawned many missionary societies, including the prominent Basel Missionary Society. Very important in terms of subsequent influence was the organization of *Innere Mission* in 1848. It is generally agreed that this movement with its extensive works of active benevolence is a direct descendant of Halle and German Pietism.

It is possible to list other denominations which have shared in the legacy of Pietism. The early Dutch Reformed communion in this country experienced a Pietist awakening through the founder of Queen's College, Theodorus J. Frelinghuysen, who had been educated by disciples of Spener and Francke. Both branches of the former Evangelical and Reformed Church are saturated with Pietist roots. The Evangelical side comes from the Prussian Pietist union of the German Lutheran and Reformed traditions in 1817. The other root, the Reformed Church, emerged from the flood of German immigrants to Pennsylvania in the first half of the eighteenth century. Its early leaders and founders were Pietists. One of the leaders, Michael Schlatter, had been a Halle student and an admirer of Untereyck, a leader of Reformed Pietism in Germany.

Philip William Otterbein, one of the German pastors invited by Schlatter, became one of the first two bishops of the United Brethren in Christ.[13] Historians and leaders in the Evangelical Mission Covenant Church of America trace their origins to Swedish Pietism and the Mission Friends.[14] Although there was no intention to lead an exodus from the state church, the transplantation to America led to a new denomination in 1885. The principal founder of the Missouri Lutheran Synod, Carl Ferdinand Wilhelm Walther, came to America in 1839. As a Leipzig student he had drunk deeply of the writings of Spener and Francke. The strictness of his Lutheran Orthodoxy, however, departed from the more latitudinarian Pietism of his day. The pluralism of attitudes within contemporary Lutheranism makes it difficult to accurately trace Pietist legacies. This is not only true of Lutheranism but of Protestantism as a whole. For this reason the above listing is in no sense exhaustive or conclusive.

Although the tremendous breadth of the legacy of Pietism points to its great impact on theology, culture, and subsequent movements, the almost infinite variety of "pietistic" currents has added to the misunderstanding of the movement. The multiplicity of connotations and great confusion are in part a result of this multi-directional legacy. Consequently, as a systematic theologian, I have appealed to my colleagues to be more judicious and temperate in their use of the word "Pietism."[15] Rather than the broad label, which is often used as a caricature of some theological tendency which is deplored, it is better to say precisely what one means. For example, if the theologian has other-worldliness or a preoccupation with private ethics in mind, it is better for him or her to name it as such. If, as theologians, we mean extreme individualism or subjectivism, why project the bogey of Pietism? If we are implying moralism, it is more helpful to name it than to apply the pietist tag.

However, as theologians and Christians in the life of the community of faith, we are so historically rooted that we will continue to apply historical labels to issues of faith and personal ways of thinking about that faith. We will not cease to use pietistic labels. For this reason we need a better understanding of what is meant historically, ecclesiologically, and theologically. Those who have negative reactions toward pietistic manifestations need to check their usage and possible caricatures with historical data and understandings in order to determine whether they are fair to those who have been called Pietists. Those who identify readily with the movement need to test their perceptions with the early movement in order to be corrected and stimulated by the early genius. In times of revival of pietist motifs and manifestations, such as the present, we need this knowledge of our predecessors to help us clarify our positions. Through more accurate understanding we will be enabled to reject what is bad and hold fast to what is good.

I share the feeling of Spener that at one time there may be more of a need for the teaching, whereas another era will call for a different theme.[16] In comparing himself with Luther, Spener spoke of the father of the Reformation as living in a day which was hungry for grace and had overrated works. Luther, therefore, spoke with vigor against the servitude of works. In place of the trust in outward works of righteousness he substituted the classical Protestant formulation of justification by faith. Spener correctly sensed that the times had changed. The ministry of his day did not have to deal with people who wanted to be blessed from good works but with people who regarded them as unnecessary and impossible.

What about our times? The nature of change is enough to erode one's confidence in exercising any gift of discernment for fear that what is written will be completely outdated by the time a book is in print. Around the middle of the century, we felt that one of the problems of American Christianity came from an overemphasis on morality and experience. This period, which in theological circles was labeled neo-orthodoxy or neo-reformation, was anti pietistic in its mood as it appealed for sound doctrine and an openness to God's revelation. Fresh interpretations and new meanings were given to old doctrines such as the doctrines of sin, revelation, justification, Christ, and the church. However, neo-orthodox theologians were often faulted for an insufficient emphasis on other doctrines such as sanctification and the Holy Spirit. In the last decade a quest has emerged for new repentance, new morality, and new life for communities of faith. Pietist themes with old and new labels, such as sanctification, the new birth, Jesus movements, house churches, the gifts and fruits of the Spirit, and communal attempts to know better times for the church before expecting better times for the world, have been very much with us. Not only at the grass roots but also in academic circles, Pietism is popular once again. My own assessment, however, is that we live in a time of such religious and cultural pluralism as to make it impossible to point to a dominant pietist mood. Our times are such that new pietist enthusiasts need to heed the warnings about the possible degenerations and dangers inherent in Pietism, while at the same time the long term and more recent critics need the theological contributions which Pietism can offer. If we as Christians wish to be in communion with our brothers and sisters in Christ, we will of necessity be concerned with and informed about pietistic issues. That part of the faith which was accented by Pietism historically will continue to flow as a part of the living stream of Christian life.

Notes

CHAPTER I

1. Paul Tillich, *A History of Christian Thought*, ed. Carl Braaten (New York: Harper and Row, 1968), p. 284.
2. Reported in Andrew Drummond, *German Protestantism Since Luther* (London: The Epworth Press, 1951), p. 79.
3. Martin Marty, *A Short History of Christianity* (Cleveland: World, 1959), p. 275.
4. F. Ernest Stoeffler, *The Rise of Evangelical Pietism* (Leiden, Holland: E. J. Brill, 1965), pp. 3ff.
5. Donald Bloesch, *Wellsprings of Renewal* (Grand Rapids: Eerdmans, 1974), pp. 12-13.
6. Philipp Jakob Spener, *Theologische Bedencken Über einige Puncten . . . 3. Die so genannten Pietisten angehende* (n.p., 1692), p. 10.
7. Spener, *Theologische Bedencken*, 4 vols. (Halle: Waysenhaus, 1715), 3:388. Hereafter cited as *T. B.*
8. John T. McNeill, *Modern Christian Movements* (Philadelphia: The Westminster Press, 1954), pp. 58-59.
9. The German poem can be found in Erich Beyreuther, *August Hermann Francke* (Marburg: Francke-Buchhandlung Gmb H., 1956), p. 67. This is my translation.
10. Translated by Martin Schmidt, "Pietism," *The Encyclopedia of the Lutheran Church*, ed. Julius Bodensieck (1965), 3:1902.
11. Egon Gerdes, "Pietism: Classical and Modern," *Concordia Theological Monthly* 39 (April, 1968), 257-268.
12. Charles Merrill Smith, *How to Become a Bishop without Being Religious* (Garden City, N. Y.: Doubleday, 1965), pp. 2-4.
13. Gerdes, "Pietism: Classical and Modern," p. 268.
14. John Howard Yoder analyzed this phrase in *The Christian Witness to the State*, Institute of Mennonite Studies Series,

no. 3 (Newton, Kansas: Faith and Life Press, 1964), pp. 84-88.

15. This is the position of F. Ernest Stoeffler in *The Rise of Evangelical Pietism*.

16. Eric Seeberg, *Mystik, Spiritualismus und die Anfänge des Pietismus im Luthertum* (Giessen: Alfred Töpelmann, 1926), p. 2.

17. See Albrecht Ritschl, *Geschichte des Pietismus* (Bonn: Adolph Marcus, 1880), 1:3-80.

18. *Ibid.*, 1:61. From some of Spener's references, certain writers trace "pietistic" elements back to this Waldensian movement of the twelfth century (see Ritschl, 1:19). The only known contact between the two movements was Spener's association with the Waldensian professor Antoine Geger at Geneva.

19. Gottfried Arnold, *Unparteyische Kirchen und Ketzer Historie*, 3 vols. (Frankfurt am Main: Thomas Fritsch, 1699-1700).

20. For more complete comparisons in Anabaptist historiography, see Guy Hershberger, ed., *The Recovery of the Anabaptist Vision* (Scottdale, Pa.: Herald Press), pp. 29-54, 105-118, 237-240. Also Robert Friedmann, *Mennonite Piety Through the Centuries* (Goshen: The Mennonite Historical Society, 1949).

21. Ernst Troeltsch, *The Social Teaching of the Christian Churches*, 2 vols., tr. Olive Wyon (New York: The Macmillan Co., 1951), 1:378ff.

22. Maurice Friedman, in foreword to Martin Buber, *Hasidism and Modern Man*, ed. and tr. by Friedman (New York: Horizon Press, 1958), p. 16.

23. Werner DeBoor, *Der Pietismus im Lutherischen Bekenntnis* (Wuppertal-Vohwinkel: Sonne und Schild, 1955), p. 4.

24. For additional biographical data on Spener see Theodore Tappert's introduction to his translation of Spener's *Pia Desideria* (Philadelphia: Fortress, 1964), pp. 8-28.
For Francke, see *Memoirs of Augustus Hermann Francke* (Philadelphia: American Sunday School Union, 1831) and Henry Guerike, *The Life of Augustus Hermann Francke*,

tr. Samuel Jackson (London: Seely and Burnside, 1837). For both, see Marie E. Richard, *Philipp Jakob Spener, August Hermann Francke* (Philadelphia: Lutheran Publication Society, 1897).

25. Carl Hildebrand von Canstein, *Ausführliche Beschreibung der Lebens-Geschichte . . . des seligen Herrn D. Philipp Jakob Speners* in Spener's *Kleine Geistliche Schrifften,* ed. J. A. Steinmetz, 2 vols. (Magdeburg, 1741), 1:16.

CHAPTER II

1. Hemme Hayen, "The Autobiography of a Seventeenth-Century Pietist," tr. and ed. by D. E. Bowan and G. M. Burnett, *The Downside Review* 87 (January, 1969), 28.

2. Spener, *Letzte Theologische Bedencken und andere Briefliche Antworten* (Halle: Waysenhaus, 1711), 3:625. *Freudigen Gewissens Frucht* (Berlin: Verlegts Johann Michael Rüdiger, 1695), pp. 4-5.

3. Paul Grünberg, *Philipp Jakob Spener* (Göttingen: Vandenhoeck und Ruprecht, 1893), 1:397.

4. Martin Schmidt, *Wiedergeburt und Neuer Mensch* (Witten: Luther-Verlag, 1969), pp. 137, 145, 146, 150. A thorough critique of Spener's position by one who represents contemporary Lutheran Orthodoxy can be found in Schmidt's essay, "Spener's Pia Desideria," in the above book, pp. 129-168.

5. Spener, *Pia Desideria,* p. 117.

6. John Friedrich Mayer, *Anti-Spenerus . . .* (Hamburg: Bey Gottfried Liebezeit, 1695), p. 9. This can be found as no. 20 of Pietist or 17th-century tracts bound in one volume and located at Union Theological Seminary.

7. Cited in Isaac Dorner, *History of Protestant Theology* (Edinburgh: T. & T. Clark, 1871), 2:211.

8. Spener, *T. B.,* 1:590.

9. For this definition see John Dillenberger and Claude Welch, *Protestant Christianity* (New York: Charles Scribner's Sons, 1954), p. 313.

10. Excellent discussion in Grünberg, *Philipp Jakob Spener*, 1:398-400.
11. Spener, *Einfältige Erklärung der Christichen Lehr* (Frankfurt: Johann David Zunner, 1702). From a current perspective, this catechism seems to be traditionally orthodox.
12. Spener, *Letzte Theologische Bedencken*, 1:349.
13. Spener, *T. B.*, 3:263.
14. Grünberg, *op. cit.*, *Philipp Jakob Spener*, 1:400-402.
15. Spener, *Letzte Theologische Bedencken*, 1:314ff.
16. Grünberg, *Philipp Jakob Spener*, 1:405-406.
17. Spener, *Letzte Theologische Bedencken*, 1:321ff.
18. Spener, *Consilia Theologia Latina* (Francofurti ad Moenum: D. Zunneri, MDCCIX), 3:794.
19. Spener, *Freudigen Gewissens Frucht*, p. 5.
20. Spener, *T. B.*, 1:373.
21. Spener, *T. B.*, 4:148ff. In this letter to a Roman Catholic priest, Spener mentions the unity of faith and love between them. But his ecumenicity did not result from confessional latitudinarianism; in the same letter he let it be known that the doctrine of the Lutheran Church is "in accordance with the simple divine Word and is not false in one article."
22. H. C. Sheldon, *The Modern Church* (Cambridge: University Press, 1889), pp. 590-591.
23. Spener, *Wenn Du Könntest Glauben* (excerpts from his writing, selected and introduced by Hans-Georg Feller; Stuttgart: J. F. Steinkopf, 1960), pp. 75-76.
24. Spener, *Pia Desideria*, p. 63.
25. Grünberg, *op. cit.*, *Philipp Jakob Spener*, 1:404-405.
26. Spener, *Wenn Du Könntest Glauben*, pp. 74-75.
27. *Ibid.*, pp. 76-77.
28. Spener, *T. B.*, 2:146; 3:649; 4:573.
29. Spener, *Wenn Du Könntest Glauben*, p. 75.
30. Erich Beyreuther, *August Hermann Francke*, pp. 127-128.
31. Quoted by Jakob Johannes Wolleb, *Gesprach zwischen einem Pietisten und einen Wiedertäufer* (1722), found in Friedmann, *Mennonite Piety*, p. 42.
32. Spener, *Pia Desideria*, p. 37.

33. Spener, *Der Klagen über das Verdorbene Christenthum Missbrauch und rechter Gebrauch* (Frankfurt am Main: Zunner, 1685).
34. Spener, *Pia Desideria*, p. 47.
35. Quoted in John T. McNeill, *A History of the Cure of Souls* (New York: Harper & Brothers, 1951), p. 183.
36. Francke, "A Letter to a Friend Concerning the Most Useful Way of Preaching," tr. David Jennings and appended to his brother's book, John Jennings, *Two Discourses* (Boston: J. Draper for J. Edward and H. Foster, 1740), p. 82.
37. Francke, *Nicodemus: or, a Treatise Against the Fear of Man* . . . (London: Joseph Downing, 1706).
38. Spener, *T. B.*, 1:159ff.
39. Spener, *Pia Desideria*, pp. 46-47.
40. Spener, *The Spiritual Priesthood*. Tr. and preface by A. G. Voigt (Philadelphia: Lutheran Publication Society, 1917), p. 15.
41. *Ibid.*, p. 17.
42. Francke, *Nicodemus,* pp. 74-75.
43. Spener, *The Spiritual Priesthood*, p. 32.
44. Quoted in Koppel A. Pinson, *Pietism as a Factor in the Rise of German Nationalism* (New York: Columbia University Press, 1934), p. 102.
45. Spener, *Pia Desideria*, p. 43.
46. *Ibid.*, p. 44.
47. *Ibid.*
48. Spener, *Kleine Geistliche Schrifften*, 1:36.
49. Spener, *T. B.*, 2:46; 1:73ff.

CHAPTER III

1. Tillich, *A History of Christian Thought*, p. 285.
2. Spener, *Consilia Theologia Latina*, 1:46.
3. Grünberg, *Philipp Jakob Spener*, 1:408.
4. Francke, *Nicodemus*, pp. 43-44.
5. Spener, *Spiritual Priesthood*, pp. 21, 34.
6. Spener, *T. B.*, 1:331; 3:338ff.
7. Spener, *Consilia Theologia Latina*, 3:144.

8. See Tadakazu Uwoke, "The Significance of Philipp Jakob Spener in the Development of Protestant Thought" (Unpublished S. T. M. thesis, Union Theological Seminary, 1924), p. 15.

9. Francke, *A Guide to the Reading and Study of the Holy Scriptures,* tr. from the Latin by William Jaques (Philadelphia: Hogan, 1823), p. 50.

10. Ludwig Fischlin, *Pietismus Deteckus* . . . (Grossen: Diacono, 1707), p. 20.

11. Spener, *Pia Desideria,* p. 46.

12. Francke, *A Guide to the Reading and Study of the Holy Scriptures,* p. 116.

13. Spener, *Erste Geistliche Schrifften* (Frankfurt am Main: Zunner, 1699), 2:122.

14. Martin Schmidt, "Spener und Luther," *Luther Jahrbuch* (Berlin: Lutherische Verlagshaus, 1957), 24:113.

15. Arthur Nagler, *Pietism and Methodism* (Nashville: Publishing House of M. E. Church, South, 1918), p. 91.

16. Francke, *A Guide to the Reading and Study of the Holy Scriptures,* pp. 66, 67, 82, 87.

17. Ph. Auguste Fischer, *Spener Comme Exégète et Son Influence comme tel Sur l'Eglise Protestante* (Strasbourg: G. Silbermann, 1862), p. 34.

18. Spener, *Spiritual Priesthood,* p. 23.

19. *Ibid.,* p. 29.

20. Francke, *Lectiones Paraeneticae,* 4 vols. (Halle: Waysenhaus, 1729-46), 4:408.

21. For a fuller discussion see Von Erhard Peschke, "Die Theologie August Hermann Franckes," found in *August Hermann Francke 1663-1963: Wort und Tat* (Berlin: Evangelische Verlagsanstalt, 1966), pp. 44-45.

22. Spener, *Spiritual Priesthood,* pp. 22-23.

23. Francke, *A Guide to the Reading and Study of the Holy Scriptures,* p. 91.

24. *Ibid.,* p. 18.

25. Spener, *T. B.,* 4:23ff.

26. Quoted in Guerike, *Life of Augustus Hermann Francke,* pp. 240-241.

27. Francke, *A Guide to the Reading and Study of the Holy Scriptures,* p. 91.

28. Spener, *Consilia Theologia Latina*, 1:260.
29. Francke, *A Guide to the Reading and Study of the Holy Scriptures*, p. 123.
30. *Ibid.*, p. 126.
31. *Ibid.*, pp. 127-128.
32. *Ibid.*, p. 129.
33. *Ibid.*, p. 130.
34. Martin Schmidt, *Wiedergeburt und Neuer Mensch*, p. 149.

CHAPTER IV

1. Spener, *Consilia Theologia Latina*, 1:28.
2. Spener, *Pia Desideria*, p. 56.
3. Spener, *Letzte Theologische Bedencken*, 1:266.
4. Spener, *T. B.*, 3:294.
5. Karl Wildenhahn, *Pictures from the Life of Spener*, tr. G. A. Wenzel (Philadelphia: J. Fred'k Smith, 1879), p. 74.
6. Martin Schmidt, "Spener und Luther," p. 123. See also his *Wiedergeburt und Neuer Mensch*, p. 192.
7. *Ibid.*, 129.
8. Spener, *T. B.*, 4:728.
9. Max Göbels, *Geschichte Des Christlischen Lebens in der Reinisch-Westphälischen Evangelischen Kirche*, 3 vols. (Coblenz: Karl Bädeker, 1849-60), 2:553.
10. Spener, *Erste Geistliche Schrifften*, p. 539.
11. Francke, "A Letter to a Friend Concerning the Most Useful Way of Preaching," p. 71.
12. Schmidt, "Spener und Luther," p. 109.
13. See Dillenberger and Welch, *Protestant Christianity*, p. 125.
14. Schmidt, "Spener und Luther," p. 126, points to Spener's usage of the plural forms of the words for sin, *Sünde, Schaden*.
15. Found in book edited by Werner Mahrholz, *Der deutsche Pietismus: Eine Auswahl von Zeugnissen, Urkunden und Bekenntnissen aus dem 17., 18. und 19. Jahrhundert* (Berlin: Furche, 1921), pp. 105-107.
16. Francke, *Faith in Christ, Inconsistent with a Sollicitous*

Concern about the Things of This World, tr. Joseph
Downing (London: Joseph Downing, 1909), pp. 1-2.

17. Francke, "A Letter to a Friend Concerning the Most Useful Way of Preaching," pp. 72-73.
18. Spener, *T. B.*, 3:140ff.
19. *Ibid.*, 2:685.
20. Spener, *Freudigen Gewissens Frucht*, p. 35.
21. *Ibid.*, p. 38.
22. Spener, *Erste Geistliche Schrifften*, p. 651.
23. Francke, *Nicodemus*, p. 98.
24. Spener, *Der Hochwichtige Articul von der Wiedergeburt* (Frankfurt am Main: Zunner, 1695), p. 20.
25. Max Göbels, *Geschichte Des Christlischen Lebens*, 2:589.
26. Spener, *Pia Desideria*, p. 63.
27. Quoted in Guerike, *Life of Augustus Hermann Francke*, p. 39.
28. Spener, *Freudigen Gewissens Frucht*, p. 41.
29. *Ibid.*, p. 52.
30. As found in Spener's *Pia Desideria*, p. 65.
31. Guerike, *Life of Augustus Hermann Francke*, p. 41.
32. Quotes from Grünberg, *Philipp Jakob Spener*, 1:452. An excellent discussion of this problem is found in this work, pp. 450-452.
33. *Ibid.*, p. 451.
34. See, for example, Schmidt, *Wiedergeburt und Neuer Mensch*, p. 186.
35. Quoted in Marie E. Richard, *Philipp Jakob Spener, August Hermann Francke*, pp. 53-54.
36. Spener, *T. B.*, 1:209.
37. Francke, "A Letter to a Friend Concerning the Most Useful Way of Preaching," p. 77.
38. Spener, *T. B.*, 1:209.
39. Grünberg, *Philipp Jakob Spener*, 1:449.
40. Spener, *Erste Geistliche Schrifften*, p. 736.
41. *Ibid.*, pt. 2, pp. 210-214.
42. *Ibid.*, pp. 204-205.
43. Spener, *Pia Desideria*, p. 80.
44. Franz Hildebrandt, *From Luther to Wesley* (London: Lutterworth Press, 1954), p. 84.
45. Spener, *T. B.*, 1:150. Having sin is *Schwachheit-Sünde*,

while doing sin is *Bossheit-Sünde.*
46. Quoted in D. Gustav Kramer, *August Hermann Francke: Ein Lebensbild,* 2 vols. (Halle: Waysenhaus, 1880-82), 1:274.
47. Spener, *Der Hochwichtige Articul von der Wiedergeburt,* pp. 6ff.
48. Spener, *Erste Geistliche Schrifften,* p. 280.
49. Spener, *Letzte Theologische Bedencken,* 1:129.
50. Grünberg, *Philipp Jakob Spener,* 1:440.
51. Francke, *A Guide to the Reading and Study of the Holy Scriptures,* p. 132.

CHAPTER V

1. Francke, *Faith in Christ,* p. 13.
2. Nagler, *Pietism and Methodism,* p. 176.
3. Joachim Lange, *Apologetische Erlauterung der Neuesten Historie bey der Evangelischen Kirche von 1689 bis 1719* . . . (Halle: Renger, 1719), p. 401.
4. Spener, *Freudigen Gewissens Frucht,* p. 46.
5. *Ibid.,* p. 23.
6. Spener, *Theologisches Bedencken über einige Puncten,* pp. 2-5.
7. Spener, *T. B.,* 1:32ff. *Consilia Theologia Latina,* 1:271.
8. Donald Bloesch, *The Evangelical Renaissance* (Grand Rapids: Eerdmans, 1973), p. 133.
9. Spener, *Pia Desideria,* pp. 116-117.
10. Spener, *T. B.,* 3:358.
11. Francke, "Anfang und Fortgang seiner Bekehrung," *Der Deutsche Pietismus,* p. 108.
12. Francke, "A Letter to a Friend Concerning the Most Useful Way of Preaching," p. 76.
13. Grünberg, *Philipp Jakob Spener,* 1:444.
14. Spener, *T. B.,* 3:71, 631.
15. Schmidt, "Spener und Luther," p. 112.
16. *Ibid.,* p. 119.
17. Spener, *Der Hochwichtige Articul von der Wiedergeburt,* p. 217.
18. Spener, *T. B.,* 1:693.

174 Understanding Pietism

19. Pinson, *Pietism as a Factor in the Rise of German Nationalism*, p. 11.

20. Theodor Geissendoerfer, "Briefe an August Hermann Francke," found in *Illinois Studies in Language and Literature* (Urbana: U. of Ill. Press, 1939), 25:160.
21. Quoted in *Memoirs of Augustus Hermann Francke*, p. 150.
22. Francke, *Nicodemus*, pp. 119, 129, 78.
23. Francke, *Pietas Hallensis*, found as an appendage to George Whitefield, *Orphan-House* (London: W. Straham, 1743), p. 88.
24. Francke in *Memoirs*, p. 146.
25. Francke, *Nicodemus*, p. 132.
26. Dorner, *History of Protestant Theology*, 2:219-220.
27. Spener, *T. B.*, 1:323-324.
28. Francke in *Memoirs*, p. 152.
29. Quoted in Kramer, *August Hermann Francke*, 1:104.
30. Max Weber, *The Protestant Ethic and the Spirit of Capitalism*, tr. R. H. Tawney (London, 1930), p. 137.
31. Francke, "Anfang und Fortgang seiner Bekehrung," *Der Deutsche Pietismus*, pp. 108-118.
32. Francke, "A Letter to a Friend Concerning the Most Useful Way of Preaching," p. 71.
33. Spener, *T. B.*, 1:56, 162ff., 197, 323ff.; 3:588.
34. Beyreuther, *August Hermann Francke*, p. 52.
35. *Ibid.*, p. 51.
36. Peschke, *Die Theologie August Hermann Francke*, p. 47.

CHAPTER VI

1. Wildenhahn, *Pictures from the Life of Spener*, pp. 28-29.
2. Spener, *Freudigen Gewissens Frucht*, p. 6.
3. Spener. Compare Kurt Aland's second edition of the *Pia Desideria* (Berlin: Walter DeGruye & Co., 1955), pp. 28-29 with Tappert's translation, *op. cit.*, pp. 58-59.
4. *Ibid.* Compare p. 28 with p. 58.
5. Francke, *Memoirs*, pp. 67-70.
6. Lange, *Apologetische Erlauterung*, p. 180.
7. Francke, *Nicodemus*, p. iii.
8. Weber, *Protestant Ethic and the Spirit of Capitalism*,

p. 62.

9. This is not to preclude the debate in biblical circles concerning the relative Greek elements in Paul's thought. It is based on the assumption, however, that Paul was more Hebraic than Greek in his anthropology.

10. Johann Arndt, *True Christianity*, tr. A. W. Boehm, 1712 (Philadelphia: The Lutheran Book Store, 1869), p. 52.

11. *Ibid.*, p. 39.

12. *Ibid.*, pp. 144-145.

13. *Ibid.*, p. 48.

14. Spener, *Wenn Du Könntest Glauben*, pp. 37-38.

15. Spener, *T. B.*, 2:392ff.

16. Beyreuther, *August Hermann Francke*, pp. 124-126.

17. James Hastings Nichols, *History of Christianity, 1650-1950* (New York: Ronald Press, 1956), p. 83.

18. Spener, *T. B.*, 3:255.

19. Quoted in Grünberg, *Philipp Jakob Spener*, 1:405.

20. Spener, *Theologische Bedencken über einige Puncten*, p. 6.

21. *Ibid.*, pp. 7-8.

22. Spener, *Freudigen Gewissens Frucht*, p. 5.

23. Spener, *Pia Desideria*, p. 52.

24. Dorner, *History of Protestant Theology*, 2:172.

25. This is the judgment of Martin Schmidt, *Wiedergeburt und Neuer Mensch*, p. 133.

26. Klaus Deppermann, *Der Hallesche Pietismus und der Preussische Staat unter Friedrich II* (Göttingen: Vandenhoeck und Ruprecht, 1961), 1:52 and *passim*.

27. Spener, *Pia Desideria*, p. 30.

28. *Ibid.*, p. 31.

29. *Ibid.*, pp. 31-32.

30. Deppermann, *Der Hallesche Pietismus*, pp. 51-58.

31. Francke, *Pietas Hallensis*, p. 61.

32. *Ibid.*, p. 104.

33. *Ibid.*, p. 77.

34. Beyreuther, *August Hermann Francke*, p. 181.

35. *Ibid.*

36. Spener, *Die Evangelische Glaubenslehre in einem Jahrgang der Predigten in Dresden, 1687* (Frankfurt am Main: Zunner, 1688), p. 1323.

37. Spener, "Selbstbiographie," *Der Deutsche Pietismus*, pp.

101-102.
38. Quoted in Richard, *Philipp Spener, Hermann Francke,* p. 148.
39. Emil Brunner, *The Divine-Human Encounter,* tr. Amandus Loos (Philadelphia: Westminster Press, 1943), p. 33.
40. Tillich, *A History of Christian Thought,* p. 284.

CHAPTER VII

1. Ritschl, *Geschichte des Pietismus.*
2. In the first chapter several contemporary Pietist scholars were listed. Here I would like to mention especially the recent work of F. Ernest Stoeffler.
3. Pinson, *op. cit. Pietism as a Factor in the Rise of German Nationalism,* p. 11.
4. Ernst Troeltsch, *Leibniz und die Anfänge des Pietismus* (Berlin: n.p., 1902).
5. Schmidt, "Spener und Luther," p. 127.
6. Drummond, *German Protestantism Since Luther,* p. 63.
7. Ruth Rouse and Stephen Neill, *A History of the Ecumenical Movement* (London: S.P.C.K., 1954), p. 101.
8. Kuno Francke, "Cotton Mather and August Hermann Francke," *Studies and Notes in Philology and Literature* (Boston: Ginn & Co., 1896), 5:61-62.
9. The recent work edited by F. Ernest Stoeffler, *Continental Pietism and Early American Christianity* (Grand Rapids: Eerdmans, 1976), makes a tremendous contribution by its sound documentation of the great influence of Pietism in American Christianity. This book helps fill the void which has long been present.
10. See Donald Durnbaugh, "The Genius of the Brethren," *Brethren Life and Thought* 4 (Winter, 1959), 31. Also read the entire article.
11. William Warren Sweet, *Religion in Colonial America* (New York: Harper & Brothers, 1903), pp. 281-282.
12. Harold Bender, in introduction to Friedmann, *Mennonite Piety,* p. vii.
13. James O. Bemesderfer, *Pietism and its Influence upon the Evangelical United Brethren Church* (Harrisburg: Evan-

gelical Press, 1966).

14. *The Covenant Quarterly* (1970), vol. 28. See especially Karl Olsson's "What Was Pietism?"

15. See my article, "The Bogey of Pietism," *The Covenant Quarterly* 25 (February, 1967), 12-17.

16. Grünberg, *Philipp Jakob Spener,* 1:523.

Index

180 *Understanding Pietism*